Elementary

New Headway
Pronunciation Course

Sarah Cunningham
Peter Moor

Contents

Introduction	*4*

Unit 1

Sounds
Introduction to consonant sounds — *6*

Word focus
The sound of English — *7*
Stress in numbers — *8*

Connected speech
Short forms (contractions) of *be* — *9*

Unit 2

Sounds
Introduction to vowel sounds (1) — *10*
Problem consonants: final '-s' — *11*
The sound /ə/ — *11*

Stress
Introduction to sentence stress — *13*

Unit 3

Sounds
Problem consonants: /r/ — *14*
Silent 'r' — *14*

Connected speech
Weak forms and linking — *16*

Intonation
Introduction to intonation: up or down? — *17*

Unit 4

Sounds
Final '-es' pronounced /ɪz/ — *18*

Stress and connected speech
Weak forms in Present Simple questions — *18*
Weak forms of *a* and *the* — *20*

Word focus
How many syllables? — *21*

Unit 5

Sounds
Introduction to vowel sounds (2) — *22*
Problem consonants: /θ/ and /ð/ ('*th*') — *23*

Intonation
Sounding polite — *24*

Unit 6

Sounds
Problem consonants: /w/ — *26*

Connected speech
can and *can't* — *27*
Pronunciation of negative forms — *28*

Unit 7

Sounds
Problem vowel sounds: /ɪ/ and /iː/ — *29*

Word focus
Past Simple forms that are difficult to pronounce — *30*

Connected speech
Hearing Past Simple forms — *31*

Stress and intonation
Intonation in *Wh-* questions — *32*

Unit 8

Sounds
Problem consonants: /dʒ/ — 33
Problem vowel sounds: /ɜː/ — 34

Connected speech
Saying dates — 35

Unit 9

Sounds
Problem vowel sounds: /æ/ and /ʌ/ — 36

Connected speech
Weak form of *of* — 37

Stress and intonation
Special stress — 38
Polite requests — 39

Unit 10

Sounds
Problem consonants: /h/ — 40

Word focus
Stress in compound nouns — 41

Connected speech
Comparatives and superlatives — 42
Short forms (contractions) — 43

Unit 11

Sounds
Introduction to diphthongs — 44
Problem consonants: /n/ and /ŋ/ — 45

Word focus
Word stress (revision) — 46

Unit 12

Sounds
Problem vowel and diphthong sounds:
/ɒ/, /ɔː/, and /əʊ/ — 47

Sounds and spelling
Words ending in the sound /ə/ — 47

Connected speech
Weak form of *to* — 48

Intonation
Sounding enthusiastic — 49

Unit 13

Sounds
Problem vowel and diphthong sounds: /e/ and /eɪ/ — 50
Problem consonants: /ʃ/ and /tʃ/ — 51

Sounds and spelling
The sound /ə/ in final syllables — 52

Connected speech
Linking (revision) — 53

Unit 14

Sounds
Problem consonants: /tʃ/, /dʒ/, and /j/ — 54
Words with similar vowel sounds — 55

Connected speech
Contractions and weak forms in the Present Perfect — 56

Phonemic symbols — 57

Key — 58

Introduction

Welcome to the *New Headway Elementary Pronunciation Course*!

The questions and answers on these pages are to help you to understand this book, so that you can get the best out of it when you use it.

Who is this book for?

The *New Headway Elementary Pronunciation Course* is for elementary students who want an introduction to English pronunciation.

How does this book work?

You can use this book (and tape/CD) on its own. The exercises in it will help you to organize your study of pronunciation.

It is also part of the *New Headway English Course* and the topics and language of each unit in this book link with those in the *New Headway Elementary Student's Book*.

Sounds exercises

		All nationalities	French	German	Greek	Hungarian	Italian	Japanese	Portuguese	Spanish	Turkish
Unit 1	Introduction to consonant sounds	✓									
Unit 2	Problem consonants: final '-s' The sound /ə/	✓ ✓									
Unit 3	Problem consonants: /r/ Silent 'r'	✓ ✓									
Unit 4	Final '-es' pronounced /ɪz/	✓									
Unit 5	Problem consonants: /θ/ and /ð/ ('th')	✓									
Unit 6	Problem consonants: /w/	✓									
Unit 7	Problem vowel sounds: /ɪ/ and /i:/		✓		✓	✓	✓		✓	✓	✓
Unit 8	Problem consonants: /dʒ/ Problem vowel sounds: /ɜ:/		✓ 	✓ ✓	✓ ✓		✓		✓ ✓	✓	✓
Unit 9	Problem vowel sounds: /æ/ and /ʌ/	✓									
Unit 10	Problem consonants: /h/		✓		✓		✓	✓	✓	✓	
Unit 11	Problem consonants: /n/ and /ŋ/	✓									
Unit 12	Problem vowel and diphthong sounds: /ɒ/, /ɔ:/, and /əʊ/	✓									
Unit 13	Problem vowel and diphthong sounds: /e/ and /eɪ/ Problem consonants: /ʃ/ and /tʃ/		✓ ✓	✓ ✓	 ✓	✓ ✓	✓ ✓			 ✓	
Unit 14	Problem consonants: /tʃ/, /dʒ/, and /j/		✓	✓	✓				✓	✓	

4

What types of exercise are there?

There are four different types of exercise in this book:

1 **Sounds** The connection between English spelling and pronunciation is often a problem for students of all nationalities. For this reason it is important to know the English sound symbols (phonemic symbols). These symbols help you to learn the pronunciation of new words easily.

   Some Sounds exercises help you to learn the phonemic symbols. As you learn them, you write an example word under each symbol from the list given under the Phonemic symbols chart on page 57. These words help you to remember the sound symbols correctly.

   Some Sounds exercises are particularly suitable for speakers of certain languages. (See the table opposite.) Sounds and spelling exercises deal with the relationship between spelling patterns and sounds. They are suitable for speakers of all languages.

2 **Connected speech** These exercises help you to pronounce words in phrases and sentences correctly.

3 **Intonation and sentence stress** These exercises help you to hear and practise different kinds of intonation and sentence stress patterns.

4 **Word focus** In these exercises you study groups of words where there are problems with sounds and word stress.

What about the recording?

This book comes with one tape or CD.

The symbol in the exercise shows exactly which part of the recording you listen to.

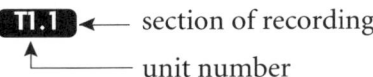

What about the key?

The answers to exercises, and tapescripts which are not in the exercises themselves, are in the key at the back of the book.

As in the *New Headway Student's Book*, sometimes we ask you questions to help you work out rules for yourself. The answers to these questions are in the key, too.

This symbol after an exercise means look at the key. The page number with the symbol shows you exactly where to look:

▶▶ p58

What about technical words?

Here is a list of technical words we use in this book.

Use a bilingual dictionary to translate them.

You can look back at this list while you use the book.

consonant	
contraction	
flat	
intonation	
linking	
phonemic	
polite	
pronunciation	
rude	
sentence	
sound	
spelling	
stress	
syllable	
symbol	
vowel	
weak	

1

Introduction to consonant sounds
The sound of English
Stress in numbers
Short forms (contractions) of *be*

Sounds

Introduction to consonant sounds

T1.1 Listen and look at the spelling.

/k/ → cake /keɪk/
/k/ → chemist's /kemɪsts/

T1.2 Look at the spelling and listen to these words.

c → /k/ cassette /kəset/
c → /s/ cigarette /sɪɡəret/

The **sound** and the **spelling** are not always the same in English. To find the pronunciation of new words, look at the phonemic symbols in your dictionary.

chemist (/ˈkemɪst/) *n.* farmacista *m./f.*; (*scientist*) chimico, a *m.*, *f.* ~ry *n.* chimica *f.*

It is important to learn the phonemic symbols.

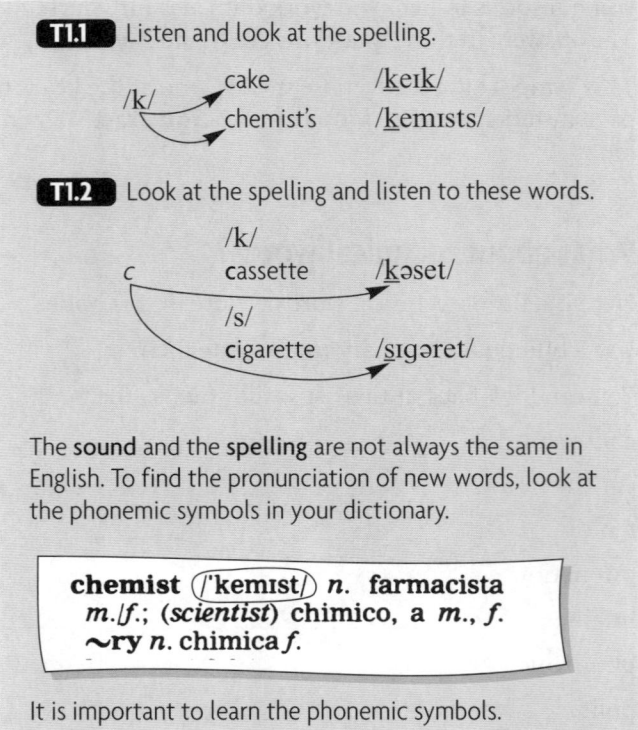

Easy consonant symbols

- /p/ pen 
- /d/ dictionary 
- /b/ book 
- /k/ camera 
- /t/ ticket 
- /g/ goal

- /f/ family
- /m/ magazine
- /v/ van
- /n/ newspaper
- /s/ stamp
- /h/ handbag
- /z/ zoo
- /r/ restaurant
- /l/ letter
- /w/ window

1 **T1.3** Listen and tick (✓) the consonant sounds that are the same in your language.

2 Which sounds are very different in your language? Are there any sounds that you don't have? Discuss your answers with your teacher.

3 Look at the phonemic symbols on page 57. Find the words from the box for sounds 1–16. Write them in the spaces under the symbols.

You will learn other consonant symbols as you work through the book.

6 Unit 1

Word focus

The sound of English

1 **T1.4** Look at the pictures below. Listen to the words in three different languages. Which is English? Tick (✓) a, b, or c.

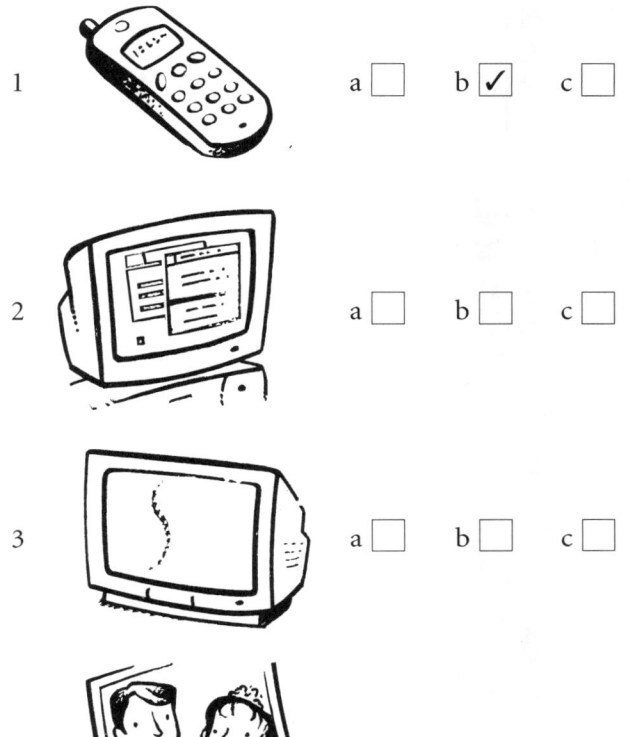

1 a ☐ b ✓ c ☐

2 a ☐ b ☐ c ☐

3 a ☐ b ☐ c ☐

4 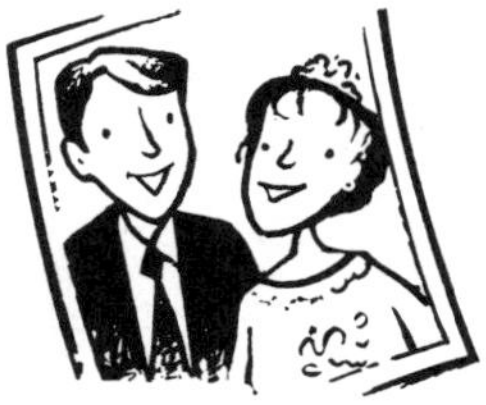 a ☐ b ☐ c ☐

5 a ☐ b ☐ c ☐

6 a ☐ b ☐ c ☐

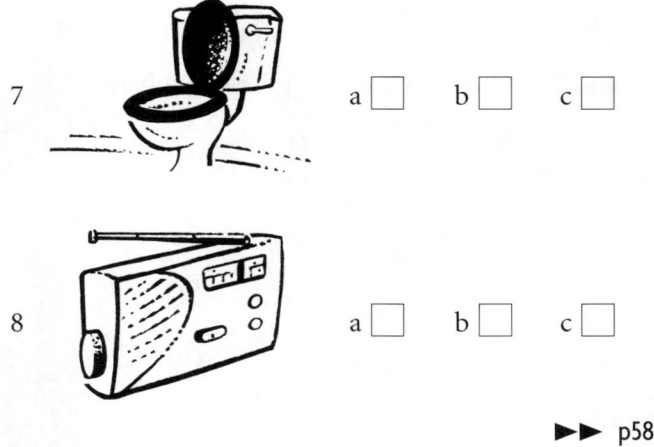

7 a ☐ b ☐ c ☐

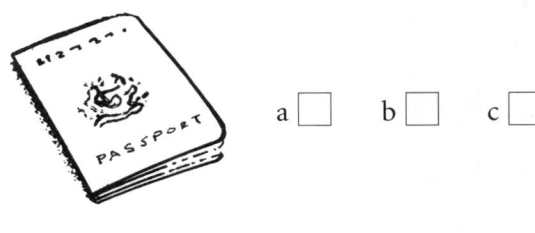

8 a ☐ b ☐ c ☐

▶▶ p58

2 **T1.5** Listen to the English words again and practise saying them.

3 Look at the stress.

• telephone • cassette • television

Listen again and mark the stress on the words below.

photograph   police   radio

passport   toilet   email

▶▶ p58

To find where the stress is on a new word, you can look at the stress mark in your dictionary.

Practise saying the words with the correct stress.

Unit 1 7

Stress in numbers

1 `T1.6` Listen to the stress in these numbers.

	• ●		● •	
13	thirteen		thirty	30
14	fourteen		forty	40
15	fifteen		fifty	50
16	sixteen		sixty	60
17	seventeen		seventy	70
18	eighteen		eighty	80
19	nineteen		ninety	90

Listen again and practise saying the numbers with the correct stress.

2 `T1.7` Choose one of the cards below, a, b or c. Listen and cross out (✗) the numbers that you hear. You will hear each number twice.

Who finishes first: a, b, or c?

a

13	60	14
50	70	15
90	18	19

b

80	16	90
15	30	14
18	17	19

c

90	13	50
14	17	16
19	40	80

3 Make a new card. You choose the numbers. Play the game again. Your teacher or another student will read out some numbers. They will be in a different order from the numbers on the recording. When you finish your card, shout *Bingo!*

▶▶ p58

Connected speech

Short forms (contractions) of *be*

1 Look at the short forms of *be* below.

I'm   (= I am)
you're   (= you are)
he's   (= he is)
she's   (= she is)
it's   (= it is)
that's   (= that is)
my name's   (= my name is)

T1.8 Listen and practise.

2 Jane is talking about her pets. Circle where the short forms go – there are seven more.

T1.9 Listen and check your answers.

▶▶ p58

3 Practise reading what Jane says, using short forms.

4 Think about your pet or an animal you know. Complete the information below.

Animal's name: _____

Animal's age: _____

Intelligent/Stupid: _____

5 Tell the other students about your pet. Use contractions!

I'm
Hello, (I am) Jane. This is my cat. Her name is Pepper. She is three years old and she is very intelligent, I think!

That is my dog, Sam. Sam is twelve years old now! He is a very nice dog, but he is very stupid!

Unit 1 9

2
Introduction to vowel sounds (1)
Problem consonants: final '-s'
The sound /ə/
Introduction to sentence stress

Sounds

Introduction to vowel sounds (1)

There are twelve vowel sounds in English.
Here are six of them.

/i:/	see	/ɪ/	sit
/u:/	do	/e/	get
/ʊ/	look	/ə/	listen

1 **T2.1** Listen and answer the questions.

1 Which sounds are long?
2 Which are the same (or very similar) in your language?
3 Which ones don't you have in your language?

▶▶ p58

Listen again and practise.

2 **T2.2** Listen to the verbs and write in the symbol for the vowel sound(s).

/ /
1 sp<u>ea</u>k

/ /
2 sp<u>e</u>ll

/ /
3 g<u>i</u>ve

/ /
7 dr<u>i</u>nk

/ / / /
4 v<u>isi</u>t

/ /
8 l<u>ea</u>ve

/ / / /
5 <u>ea</u>t

/ /
9 c<u>oo</u>k

/ /
6 r<u>ea</u>d

/ /
10 sw<u>i</u>m

▶▶ p58

Listen again and practise saying the verbs.

10   Unit 2

3 Look at the phonemic symbols on page 57. Find the words from the box for sounds 25, 26, 27, 32, 33, and 36. Write them in the spaces under the symbols.

You will learn the other vowel symbols in Unit 5.

Problem consonants: final '-s'

A lot of words end in -s in English.

1 **Plural nouns**
cups /s/
pens
stamps

2 **he/she Present Simple forms**
speaks
reads
loves

3 **Possessives**
Anna's friend
Jane's bag
Pete's mum

4 **Contraction of *is***
It's here.
How's Andy?
He's okay.

⚠ The final -s is **always** pronounced in English.

Sometimes the sound is /s/.
　　　　　　/s/
Example cups

Sometimes the sound is /z/.
　　　　　　/z/
Example pens

1 **T2.3** Listen to the words and phrases above. Write in the pronunciation of -s: /s/ or /z/.

▶▶ p58

2 Listen again and practise saying the words.

The sound /ə/

1 **T2.4** Are these food words the same in your language? Listen to the pronunciation in English.

One sound is very important – the sound /ə/.
　　　　　　　/ə/
Example hamburger

This is the most frequent vowel sound in English. It is in weak or unstressed syllables.

2 Listen again and mark the /ə/ sounds and stress like this.

● 　/ə/
hamburger

▶▶ p58

Listen again and practise saying the words.

3 Match the words to the pictures.

1. ☐ potato ___
2. ☐ pepper ___
3. ☐ yoghurt ___
4. ☐ chicken ___
5. ☐ tuna ___
6. ☐ orange ___
7. ☐ banana ___
8. ☐ chocolate ___
9. ☐ coffee ___
10. ☐ sandwich ___

▶▶ p58

4 **T2.5** Listen and tick (✓) the words that have an /ə/ sound.

▶▶ p58

5 Listen again and mark the stress.

▶▶ p58

6 Practise saying the words.

12 Unit 2

Stress

Introduction to sentence stress

1 **T2.6** The computer is asking Jack some questions. Listen.

In Jack's answers some words are strong and some words are weak. The important words are strong. The others are weak.

☐ ■
My name's Jack.

2 Practise Jack's answers, like this.

mm MM MM	☐ ■ My name's Jack.
mm mm MM	■ I'm from Leeds.
mm mm mm-MM-mm	■ I'm a mechanic.

mm MM-mm	■ I'm twenty.
MM mm MM	☐ ■ No, I'm not.

⚠ It is important to use strong and weak words like Jack, or you will sound like the computer!

3 **T2.7** Look at the computer's questions. Which are the important (strong) words? Listen to a real person asking the questions and mark the strong words.

☐ ■
What's your name?

▶▶ p58

4 Listen again and practise the questions. Then practise the questions and answers with a partner.

Unit 2 13

3

Problem consonants: /r/
Silent 'r'
Weak forms and linking
Introduction to intonation: up or down?

Sounds

Problem consonants: /r/

1 **T3.1** Listen to the sound /r/. Is it the same in your language?

Rolls Royce

the River Rhine

right and wrong

rock 'n' roll

a red, red rose

2 Listen again and practise saying the phrases.

Silent 'r'

Look.

children	= letter r + vowel sound	= /r/
surname	= letter r + consonant sound	= r̶
mother	= letter r + nothing	= r̶

> ⚠ are = /ɑː/
> aren't = /ɑːnt/
> The e is silent.

1 **T3.2** Listen to these examples.

r + vowel sound	r + consonant sound or nothing
boyfriend	sister
Granny	father
married	first name

Practise saying the words and phrases.

14 Unit 3

2. Cross out (✗) the *r*s that are not pronounced in the words below.

T3.3 Listen and check your answers.

▶▶ p58

Practise saying the words.

3. Work with a partner. Write five words with *r*s that are pronounced, and five words with *r*s that are **not** pronounced.

▶▶ p58

Connected speech

Weak forms and linking

1 Match the word in **A** to the opposite in **B**.

A	B
get up	finish
open	leave
arrive	go to bed
start	close

▶▶ p59

2 **T3.4** Listen and count the words you hear. (*o'clock* = one word)

1. [6] _____ bank opens _____.
2. [ ] He goes _____ seven _____.
3. [ ] This office _____ half past two.
4. [ ] We get up _____ o'clock.
5. [ ] Her plane _____ two fifteen.
6. [ ] The programme _____ about _____ thirty.
7. [ ] The film _____ at half _____.
8. [ ] My train _____ about _____.

▶▶ p59

3 Listen again and write in the missing words.

▶▶ p59

4 When we speak fast, we make some words weak. The weak words often have the sound /ə/.

/ə/ /ə/
at nine o'clock

The weak words are not stressed.

T3.5 Practise saying these times. Use the weak forms.

/ət/ /ə/
at nine o'clock

/ət/ /ə/
at two o'clock

/ət/ /ə/
at seven o'clock
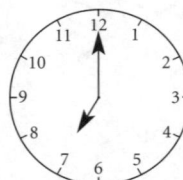

/ət/ /ə/
at twelve o'clock

/ət/ /ə/
at three o'clock
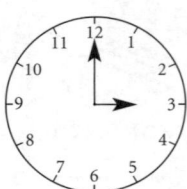

/ət/ /ə/
at five o'clock

5 When we speak fast, we also link words together. We do this when one word ends with a consonant sound and the next word begins with a vowel sound.

The bank_opens_at nine_o'clock.

Here are some more examples. Practise saying them.

He goes to bed_at seven_o'clock.

This_office closes_at half past two.

We get_up_at_about_eight_o'clock.

6 Look at sentences 5–8 in 2 above. Find the words that link together.

▶▶ p59

7 Practise saying all the sentences. Speak fast, using weak forms and linking.

Intonation

Introduction to intonation: up or down?

1 **T3.6** Listen to the pairs of words below. One is a question. Write **.** next to the statements, and **?** next to the questions.

1	Okay	·	Okay	?
2	Bill	☐	Bill	☐
3	Yes	☐	Yes	☐
4	Coffee	☐	Coffee	☐

▶▶ p59

2 We know these words are questions because the intonation goes **up**.

Okay?

The other words are **not** questions. The intonation goes **down**.

Okay.

Is this the same in your language?

Listen again and repeat. Pay attention to the up and down intonation.

3 Work with a partner. Say the words below. Sometimes use question intonation () and sometimes use statement intonation (). Your partner must say if you are asking a question.

Sorry? as a question = Say it again.

| Milk | Here | Really | No | Sorry* | Anne | Ready |

Unit 3   17

4

Final '-es' pronounced /ɪz/
Weak forms in Present Simple questions
Weak forms of *a* and *the*
How many syllables?

Sounds

Final '-es' pronounced /ɪz/

The final -es is pronounced /ɪz/ after:

-s or -ss /s/	-sh /ʃ/	-ch /tʃ/
kisses	washes	matches
buses	pushes	churches

-x /ks/	-z /z/	-ge /dʒ/
boxes	Liz's	pages
mixes	houses*	oranges

⚠ *Note   house = /haʊs/
              houses = /haʊzɪz/

1 **T4.1** Listen and practise saying the words above.

2 Work with a partner.

    Student A   Look at card **A** on p19.

    Student B   Look at card **B** on p20.

Read each word to your partner. Your partner must say the word with -s at the end (pronounced /z/ or /ɪz/).

You can check the answers at the bottom of the card.

Stress and connected speech

Weak forms in Present Simple questions

1 **T4.2** Listen to the dialogues and write in **B**'s answers.

1

2

3

18   Unit 4

4

5

6

▶▶ p59

> In fast speech *Do you* is often pronounced /dʒə/.
>
> /dʒə/
> Do you know the time?
>
> /dʒə/
> Do you have a light?
>
> /dʒə/
> Do you speak English?

2 **T4.3** Practise the questions. Start with the strong words, like this:

  ☐ ■
 know the time?

 /jə/ ☐ ■
 you know the time?

 /dʒə/ ☐ ■
 Do you know the time?

3 Practise the other questions in the same way. Practise the dialogues with a partner. Pronounce *Do you* correctly.

4 Look at the questions below. Check the meaning of new words in your dictionary or with your teacher. Practise saying the questions, pronouncing *Do you* correctly.

> 1 Where do you live?
> 2 Do you live with your parents?
> 3 Do you have any children?
> 4 Do you like learning English?
> 5 Do you study English a lot at home?
> 6 Do you speak other languages?
> 7 What do you do in your spare time?
> 8 Do you smoke?
> 9 Do you like sport?
> 10 What sort of music/books/films do you like?

5 Choose five of these questions. Decide who you want to ask. All stand up and ask each other.

CARD A (see p18)

1 live	4 job	7 day
2 love	5 teach	8 nurse
3 language	6 drive	9 office

CARD A

1 /z/ 2 /z/ 3 /ɪz/
4 /z/ 5 /ɪz/ 6 /z/
7 /z/ 8 /ɪz/ 9 /ɪz/

Unit 4   19

Weak forms of *a* and *the*

1 Margaret is talking to her new colleague, Shirley, about her family. You can see their conversation below, but the words *a* and *the* are not there. Read the conversation, and put in eight *a*s and two *the*s.

M Do you have children, Shirley?
S Yes, **a** son and **a** daughter.
M Oh, that's nice, what do they do?
S My daughter Jenny's music teacher, and Michael, my son, is at college – he wants to be pilot!
M Oh, lovely!
S Yes …
M Do they live at home?
S Michael lives with me, but Jenny lives in London – she's married with two children.
M Oh! So you're grandmother!
S Yes, she has girl and boy too – Rebecca and Thomas.
M Oh, lovely – how old are they?
S girl's seven and boy's two – do you want to see photo?
M Oh yes … Ah … aren't they beautiful!

T4.4 Listen and check your answers.

▶▶ p59

2 *a* and *the* are nearly always pronounced as **weak** forms. They have the vowel sound /ə/.

/ə/	/ðə/
a girl	the girl
/ə/	/ðə/
a boy	the boy

T4.5 Practise saying the phrases below. Pronounce *a* and *the* correctly.

1 a girl   a boy
   a daughter   a son
   She's a music teacher. He wants to be a pilot.
2 the girl   the boy
   the daughter the son

3 Look at the dialogue again. Some words are strong (stressed).

   ☐ ■ ☐
   Do you **have** children, Shirley?

   ☐ ■
   Yes, a **son** and a **daughter**.

   These are the important words.

4 Practise saying the dialogue line by line. Pay attention to the stress, and the pronunciation of *a* and *the*. Read the dialogue aloud with a partner.

5 Work with a partner. Have a similar conversation about your families. Pay attention to the pronunciation of *a* and *the*.

CARD B (see p18)

1 class	4 catch	7 come
2 arrive	5 doctor	8 leave
3 sandwich	6 address	9 village

1 /ɪz/   2 /z/   3 /ɪz/
4 /ɪz/   5 /z/   6 /ɪz/
7 /z/   8 /z/   9 /ɪz/

CARD B

20 Unit 4

Word focus

How many syllables?

1 Use these clues to complete the crossword above. Use your dictionary to check spelling.

   Across →
   2 the opposite of boring
   3 brown and sweet, children love it
   4 You can buy lunch or dinner here.
   6 potatoes, carrots, peas, cabbage
   9 You use it to find the meaning of new words.
   10 the month after January

   Down ↓
   1 the day before Thursday
   3 You use it to take photos.
   5 not single – has a husband/wife
   7 all, each
   8 military man

   T4.6 Listen and check your answers.

   ▶▶ p59

   In English, some words have 'silent syllables'.
   interesting = / ɪn|trəs|tɪŋ/ = three syllables

2 Look at these words from the crossword. How many syllables are there in each word? Listen again and check.

camera	every	married	vegetables
chocolate	February	restaurant	Wednesday
dictionary	interesting	soldier	

   ▶▶ p59

3 Which syllable is silent? Cross out the 'silent syllables' and mark the stress like this.

   •
   intresting

   ▶▶ p59

4 Practise saying the words. Don't put in any extra syllables!

5 Here are some more words with 'silent syllables'. How many syllables are there in each word?

   1 aren't   4 comfortable
   2 evening   5 family
   3 favourite   6 secretary

   ▶▶ p59

6 Practise saying the words.

7 Practise saying the phrases below.

   my favourite chocolate

   every Wednesday evening

   What an interesting camera!

   Are you comfortable?

   They aren't married.

Unit 4   21

5 Introduction to vowel sounds (2)
Problem consonants: /θ/ and /ð/ ('*th*')
Sounding polite

Sounds

Introduction to vowel sounds (2)

1 **T5.1** Listen to the other six vowel sounds.

/ɜː/ word ___curtain___
/ɔː/ four _____
/æ/ man _____
/ʌ/ bus _____
/ɑː/ part _____
/ɒ/ shop _____

2 Practise saying the sounds. Cover the words. Can you remember the word for each sound?

3 **T5.2** Listen to the vowel sounds in the words below.

c<u>ar</u>pet

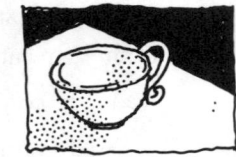
c<u>u</u>p

l<u>a</u>mp

p<u>o</u>ts

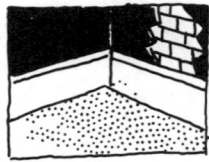
w<u>a</u>ll

c<u>ur</u>tain

Write the words next to the correct symbol in 1.

▶▶ p59

4 Below are some more 'home' words. Match the phonemic symbols with the pictures below.

1 /frɪdʒ/   **h**   6 /mɪrə/
2 /dɔː/   7 /kʊkə/
3 /gɑːdən/   8 /lɪvɪŋ ruːm/
4 /bɑːθ/   9 /telɪvɪʒən/
5 /kʌbəd/   10 /wɒʃɪŋ məʃiːn/

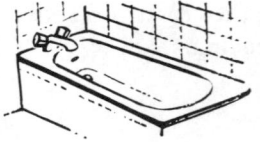
a

f

b

g

c

d

h **fridge**

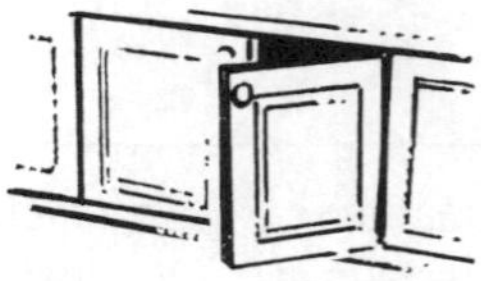

e

i

j

T5.3 Listen and check your answers.

▶▶ p59

22 Unit 5

5 Practise saying the words, paying attention to the pronunciation of the vowel sounds.

6 Look at the phonemic symbols on page 57. Find the words from the box for sounds 28, 29, 30, 31, 34, and 35. Write them in the spaces under the symbols.

Problem consonants: /θ/ and /ð/ ('th')

1 **T5.4** Listen. A lot of English words are spelt with *th*. These letters are pronounced /θ/ or /ð/.

/θ/	/ð/
three	this
thirty	that
thousand	these
both	those
theatre	there

To make these sounds, the tongue must touch the back of your teeth like this.

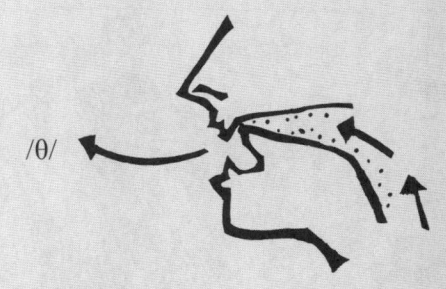

If you have problems with the sounds, put your finger in front of your mouth and touch it with your tongue, like this.

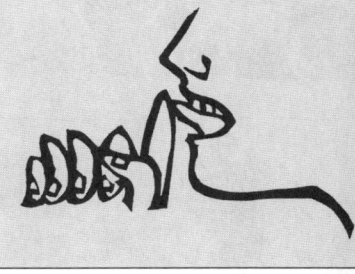

⚠ With the sound /ð/ you use your voice. With /θ/ you do not use your voice.

2 Listen again and practise saying the words.

3 Work in groups of three.

Write eight words spelt with *th* (not the words above). Are they pronounced /θ/ or /ð/? Use your dictionary to check.

The first group to finish shouts *Stop!* The winning group reads out their words. If they pronounce a word incorrectly, the other groups can shout *Challenge!*

4 **T5.5** Look at the pictures and listen.

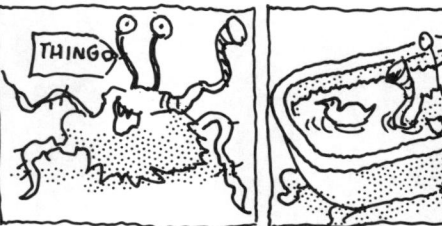

1 This is a Thing.   2 This is a Thing having a bath.

3 This is a Thing with his three brothers.

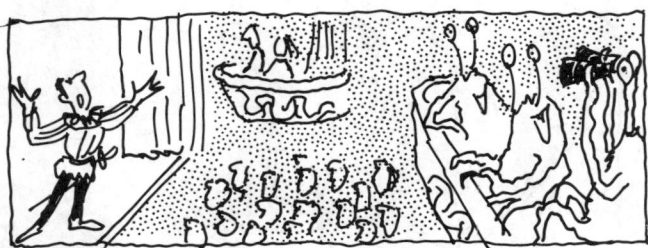

4 Three Things together at the theatre

5 This Thing's thirtieth birthday

Read the sentences. Pay attention to the *th* sounds!

5 Look at the phonemic symbols on page 57. Find the words from the box for sounds 18 and 19. Write them in the spaces under the symbols.

Intonation

Sounding polite

1 **T5.6** Listen to the people in Office A and the people in Office B.

Why do the people in Office B **sound** more friendly? Do you use intonation like this in your language? Do you think it is important?

2 In English it is very important to use intonation to sound polite and friendly. Look at the difference between the voices in Office A and Office B.

3 Listen again and practise the polite, friendly intonation of Office B.

4 Look at the picture of the Tourist Information Office. Below the picture are the lines of three conversations. Write each line in the correct speech bubble.

Desk 1

Yes, please. Is the Museum of Modern Art near here?

Hello. Can I help you?

Mmm, just a minute ... here's a map ...

Desk 2

Sorry, we don't have information about hotels. Try next door.

Next, please.

Hello, can you help me? I want a hotel for three nights.

Thank you.

Desk 3

Sure, on the left opposite the underground station.

Yes, sir?

Excuse me ...

Is there a bookshop near here?

T5.7 Listen and check your answers.

 p59

5 Practise saying the dialogues line by line. Copy the polite intonation. Practise the dialogues with a partner.

Unit 5   25

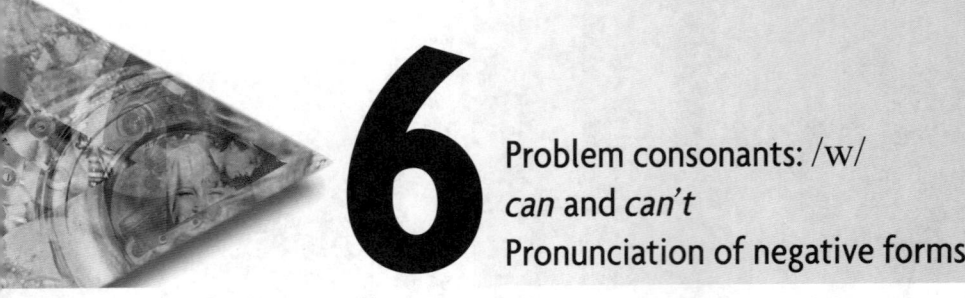

6 Problem consonants: /w/
can and can't
Pronunciation of negative forms

Sounds

Problem consonants: /w/

1 **T6.1** Listen to the sentences. Underline the /w/ sounds.

2 Do you have the sound /w/ in your language?
Try starting with /u:/.

uuu ... where   uuu ... was
uu ... where   uu ... was
u ... where   u ... was
where   was

3 Practise saying the sentences in 1. Start very slowly, then say them faster and faster.

4 Match the words in the box with the phonemic symbols below.

when 9	who	swim	what
week 8	winter	whole	twenty
wrong	we	two	write

1 /wi:/   5 /rɒŋ/   9 /wen/
2 /tu:/   6 /raɪt/   10 /swɪm/
3 /hu:/   7 /'twenti/   11 /həʊl/
4 /'wɪntə/   8 /wi:k/   12 /wɒt/

▶▶ p59

5 Find five words in the box with a silent *w*. Underline them.

▶▶ p59

6 Find another example in the box to complete the rules below.

Rule	Examples
1 *w* before *r* is silent.	write, _____
2 *wh* and *o*: *w* is silent.	who, _____

▶▶ p59

7 **T6.2** Listen and practise saying the silent *w* words.

Connected speech

can and *can't*

1 **T6.3** Listen to two children, Ben and Isabel, talking about what they can and can't do. Put ticks (✓) or crosses (✗) in the table.

	1 Ben	2 Isabel	3 you	4 your partner
play football	✓			
use a computer				
swim 100 metres				
ride a bicycle				
ride a horse				
sew				
speak French				
play the piano				
run fast				

▶▶ p60

> **T6.4** Notice the pronunciation and stress:
>
> /kən/   /kɑːnt/
> ☐ ☐   ■ ☐ ☐
> I can ride a bicycle   but   I can't ride a horse

2 **T6.5** Listen and practise saying these sentences.
1 I can speak English. I can't speak Chinese.
2 I can play football. I can't play tennis.
3 I can drive a car. I can't drive a lorry.
4 I can read fast. I can't write fast.

3 Look back at the table in 1. Which of the things can you do? Complete column 3.

4 Practise saying the sentences carefully so that your teacher can understand!

I can't play football. I can ride a bicycle.

5 Work with a partner. Tell your partner which things you can and can't do. Listen to the things your partner can and can't do. Complete column 4.

Pronunciation of negative forms

1 **T6.6** Listen to the dialogue. Do not write in the verbs. Tick (✓) the affirmative verbs, and cross (✗) the negatives.

Bob My mother's parents, Thomas and Frida, _____ (1 ✓) a strange couple. They _____ (2 ☐) married nearly sixty years. They _____ (3 ☐) very rich, but they _____ (4 ☐) very happy.

Jack Why?

Bob Frida _____ (5 ☐) English … she _____ (6 ☐) speak English very well.

Jack Where _____ (7 ☐) she from?

Bob Berlin … Germany.

Jack _____ (8 ☐) Thomas speak German?

Bob Well, he _____ (9 ☐) speak many languages, but he _____ (10 ☐) speak German.

Jack That's strange! And what about your mother? _____ (11 ☐) she speak German?

Bob Well, she _____ (12 ☐) understand it very well, but she _____ (13 ☐) really speak it.

▶▶ p60

2 Listen again and fill in the correct verb form: *was/wasn't; were/weren't; can/can't; could/couldn't.*

▶▶ p60

3 When we speak fast, we use contractions and weak forms for these verbs.

T6.7 Listen and practise.

1 was = /wəz/
Where was she from?

2 wasn't = /wɒznt/
She wasn't English.

3 were = /wə/
They were very rich.

4 weren't = /wɜ:nt/
They weren't very happy.

5 can = /kən/
She can understand it.

6 can't = /kɑ:nt/
She can't speak it.

7 could = /kəd/
He could speak many languages.

8 couldn't = /kʊ(d)nt/
He couldn't speak German.

4 Practise saying the dialogue line by line, paying attention to the pronunciation of these verb forms. Practise the dialogue with a partner.

7

Problem vowel sounds: /ɪ/ and /i:/
Past Simple forms that are difficult to pronounce
Hearing Past Simple forms
Intonation in *Wh-* questions

Sounds

Problem vowel sounds: /ɪ/ and /i:/

1 Look at the words below. Check the meaning of new words in your dictionary or with your teacher.

/ɪ/ /i:/

1 (sit)   seat

2 hit   heat

 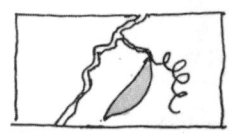

3 bin   bean

4 ship   sheep

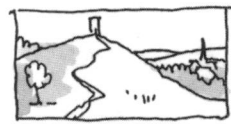 

5 hill   heel

6 lick   leak

2 **T7.1** Listen and circle the word in 1 you hear twice.

▶▶ p60

3 /ɪ/ is a **short** sound. To make it your lips look like this.

/ɪ/

/i:/ is a **long** sound. To make it your lips look like this.

/i:/

Practise saying the pairs of words.

4 **T7.2** Look at the words below. Listen to the instructions on the recording and join the words with lines. You will make a letter of the alphabet. What is it?

eat •   • live   • cheap   • hit

• leave   • it   • wheel   • will

chip •   • heat   • fill   • feel

• hill   seat •   sit •   heel •

bin •   ship •   bean •   • sheep

fit •   • feet   • leak   • lick

▶▶ p60

Unit 7   29

Word focus

Past Simple forms that are difficult to pronounce

1 Look at the verbs below. Check the meaning of new words in your dictionary or with your teacher. Write in the past form.

   1 read   **read**   6 hear   _____
   2 learn _____   7 buy   _____
   3 run   _____   8 say   _____
   4 fall   _____   9 teach _____
   5 see   _____   10 think _____

   ▶▶ p60

2 Can you pronounce the past forms?

   > You can find the pronunciation in your dictionary.
   >
   > 1 **read** /riːd/ *verb* (**reads**, **reading**, **read** (red), **has read**)
   > 1 look at words and understand them: *Have you read this book? It's very interesting.*

   Look at the phonemic transcription of *read*. Can you pronounce it?

3 Can you pronounce the past forms below?

   > 2 **learn** /lɜːn/ *verb* (**learns**, **learning**, **learnt** (lɜːnt) or **learned** (lɜːnd), **has learnt** or **has learned**)
   > 1 find out something, or how to do something, by studying or by doing it often:

   > 3 **run**¹ /rʌn/ *verb* (**runs**, **running**, **ran** (ræn), **has run**)
   > 1 move very quickly on your legs: *I was late so I ran to the bus-stop.*
   > 2 go; make a journey: *The buses don't run*

   > 4 **fall**¹ /fɔːl/ *verb* (**falls**, **falling**, **fell** (fel), **has fallen** /ˈfɔːlən/)
   > 1 go down quickly; drop: *The book fell off the table.* ◇ *She fell down the stairs and broke her arm.*

   > 5 **see** /siː/ *verb* (**sees**, **seeing**, **saw** (sɔː), **has seen** /siːn/)
   > 1 know something using your eyes: *It was so dark that I couldn't see anything.* ◇ *Can you see that plane?* ◇ *I'm going to*

   > 6 **hear** /hɪə(r)/ *verb* (**hears**, **hearing**, **heard** (hɜːd), **has heard**)
   > 1 get sounds with your ears: *Can you hear that noise?* ◇ *I heard somebody laughing in the next room.*

   T7.3 Listen and check your answers. Practise saying the past forms.

4 Match the verbs in the box to their past forms below.

see	read	wear	pay	say
think	buy	put	teach	mean
catch	cut	send		

   1 saw   _____   wore   _____ ✓
   2 read   _____   said   _____ ☐
   3 said   _____   paid   _____ ☐
   4 caught _____   taught _____ ☐
   5 thought _____   bought _____ ☐
   6 sent   _____   meant   _____ ☐
   7 cut   _____   put   _____ ☐

5 **T7.4** Listen to the pairs of verbs in 4. Tick (✓) the box if the past forms rhyme, put a cross (✗) if they don't.

   ▶▶ p60

6 Practise saying the past forms above. Test a partner. You say a verb from the box in 4 and your partner says the past form.

30 Unit 7

Connected speech

Hearing Past Simple forms

> **T7.5** -ed at the end of regular Past Simple forms is pronounced in three different ways. Listen.
>
> | /t/ | /d/ | /ɪd/ |
> |---|---|---|
> | liked | loved | hated |
> | worked | lived | intended |
> | finished | opened | started |
> | stopped | arrived | ended |

1 Practise saying the verbs in the three groups above.

2 Complete the rule.

> The -ed ending is pronounced /ɪd/ if the infinitive of the verb ends with the sound / / or / /.

▶▶ p60

3 **T7.6** In a sentence the -ed form is sometimes difficult to hear. Listen to the five pairs of sentences below. Can you hear the difference between a (Present Simple) and b (Past Simple)?

1 a We like her.
  b We liked her.

2 a I love him.
  b I loved him.

3 a They hate it.
  b They hated it.

4 a I want that.
  b I wanted that.

5 a They enjoy their English lessons.
  b They enjoyed their English lessons.

Listen again and practise saying the pairs of sentences.

4 **T7.7** Listen to the sentences and circle the verb you hear, Present Simple or Past Simple.

1 We arrive/(arrived) on Monday morning.
2 It opens/opened at nine o'clock.
3 I finish/finished work on Friday afternoon at six o'clock.
4 They close/closed on Monday.
5 They start/started at eight o'clock.
6 The trains stop/stopped at midnight.

▶▶ p60

5 **T7.8** Close your book. Listen and practise saying each sentence in the Past Simple. Pay attention to the pronunciation of the -ed ending.

Unit 7   31

Stress and intonation

Intonation in *Wh-* questions

1 **T7.9** You will hear the *beginning* of seven questions. Listen and tick (✓) the correct words below to finish the questions. There is only **one** correct answer.

1. ☐ a ... you born?
   ☐ b ... did you born?
   ✓ c ... were you born?

2. ☐ a ... born your sister?
   ☐ b ... your sister born?
   ☐ c ... you born?

3. ☐ a ... married?
   ☐ b ... born?
   ☐ c ... birthday?

4. ☐ a ... her grandfather die?
   ☐ b ... die her grandfather?
   ☐ c ... her grandfather died?

5. ☐ a ... was he?
   ☐ b ... he was?
   ☐ c ... he did?

6. ☐ a ... went to university?
   ☐ b ... were to university?
   ☐ c ... go to university?

7. ☐ a ... you leave university?
   ☐ b ... you were left university?
   ☐ c ... you left university?

2 **T7.10** Listen to the full questions and their replies. Check your answers.

▶▶ p60

3 In *Wh-* questions (questions with *What*, *Who*, *When*, *Where*, *Why*, *How*, etc.) the intonation usually goes **down** on the main stress, not up.

Where were you born?

When was your sister born?

⚠ If your intonation is **flat** you may sound **rude**.

T7.11 It helps **to start** the question quite **high**.

Where were you born?

Where were you born?

Where were you born?

Practise saying the other questions in the same way.

4 ◀ **T7.10** Work with a partner. Look at the tapescript on page 60. Practise reading the dialogue together.

32   Unit 7

8
Problem consonants: /dʒ/
Problem vowel sounds: /ɜː/
Saying dates

Sounds

Problem consonants: /dʒ/

1 **T8.1** Listen to the sound /dʒ/ in these names.

Do you have this sound in your language?

> The sound /dʒ/ is made with the two sounds /d/ and /ʒ/. First say /d/. Then say /ʒ/.
>
> Repeat each sound quickly until you say the two sounds together. You use your voice. Feel your throat vibrate when you say it.

Listen again and practise saying the names.

2 Below are some famous people with the sound /dʒ/ in their names. Who are they? Use the photos to help.

1 /dʒɒn 'lenən/

4 /dʒɔːdʒ 'kluːni/

2 /mɪk 'dʒægə/

5 /'dʒuːlɪə 'rɒbəts/

3 /'dʒæki 'kenədi/

6 /dʒɔːdʒ 'maɪkəl/

▶▶ p60

Practise saying their names.

3 Look at the phonemic symbols on page 57. Find the word from the box for sound 23. Write it in the space under the symbol.

Unit 8 33

Problem vowel sounds: /ɜː/

1 **T8.2** Listen to the words below. They all have the sound /ɜː/.

work	learn	girl	first
nurse	world	third	her
heard	word		

The vowel sound is spelt in many ways but all of the words have an *r*. Is the *r* pronounced?

▶▶ p60

2 **T8.3** Listen to some longer words and underline the /ɜː/ sound. Which three words don't have an /ɜː/ sound?

Thursday	Saturday	birthday
personal	journalist	journey
university	restaurant	hamburger
Germany	conversation	thirtieth

▶▶ p60

3 The sound /ɜː/ is made in the middle of the mouth. The lips are relaxed.

/ɜː/ is a **long** sound.

Listen again and practise saying the words in 1 and 2 above.

4 **T8.4** Look at the newspaper headlines below. Check the meaning of new words in your dictionary or with your teacher. Listen to the headlines one by one. How many /ɜː/ sounds are there? Write the number in the box.

1 ☐

Nurse Kirsty marries in Turkey

2 ☐

Prince Albert's thirtieth birthday

3 ☐

GERMAN UNIVERSITY BURNS

4 ☐

British workers 'worst in world'

5 ☐

▶▶ p60

Listen again and practise saying the headlines.

Connected speech

Saying dates

1 Look at the words below. Check the meaning of new words in your dictionary or with your teacher.

saint	lovers	destroy
parliament	war	joke
witch	official	celebrate

2 **T8.5** Below are the names of some special days in Britain. You will hear when they are, and what they celebrate. Listen and write in when they are.

1 St Valentine's Day **14 February** 3 St George's Day

2 April Fool's Day   4 The Queen's Birthday

5 Halloween   7 Remembrance Sunday

6 Guy Fawkes Night   8 St Andrew's Day

▶▶ p61

Which ones do you celebrate in your country too?

3
We *write* dates like this.

14 February   1 April

We *say* dates like this.

/ðə/   /əv/
the fourteenth of February

/ðə/   /əv/
the first of April

We use the **weak** forms of *the* and *of* when we say dates. Notice the linking when we speak fast. (See Unit 3.)

/fɔːtiːnθəv/   /fɜːstəveɪprəl/
the fourteenth‿of February   the first‿of‿April

T8.6 Listen to the dates above again. Practise saying them, with the weak forms and linking.

▶▶ p61

4 Write down five dates that are important in your country. Practise saying them correctly. Why are they important?

Unit 8 35

9
Problem vowel sounds: /æ/ and /ʌ/
Weak form of *of*
Special stress
Polite requests

Sounds

Problem vowel sounds: /æ/ and /ʌ/

1 **T9.1** Listen to the vowel sounds in the words below. Can you hear the difference?

2 **T9.2** Listen to the food words below. Write them on the correct bag in 1.

jam	h*o*ney	c*a*bbage	b*u*tter
bun	*a*pple	c*a*rrot	s*a*lad
*o*nion	m*u*shroom	ham	cuc*u*mber

3 **T9.3** Listen and check your answers.

▶▶ p61

4 Complete the rule.

> 1 The sound /æ/ is spelt with the letter _____.
>
> 2 The sound /ʌ/ is usually spelt with the letter _____ but sometimes with the letter _____.

▶▶ p61

5 Listen again to the first part. Practise saying the words from Bag 1 above.

6 Now listen to the second part. Practise saying the words from Bag 2 above.

7 **T9.4** Listen to the dialogue below. Check the meaning of new words in your dictionary or with your teacher.

Daughter Mum ... what have we got for supper?

Mum Sorry, there's not much ... ham ... scrambled eggs ... or there's some mushroom salad left.

Daughter I'll just have bread and jam ... have we got any butter?

Mum Sorry, love. There's none left.

Daughter Oh, Mum! There's nothing I want!

Mum Well, have a nice cup of hot chocolate.

Daughter Mm ... **you** make lovely hot chocolate ... Thanks, Mum!

8 Work with a partner. Find all the words in the dialogue that have an /æ/ or an /ʌ/ sound. Listen again and check your answers.

▶▶ p61

9 Practise saying the dialogue line by line, pronouncing the two sounds correctly. Practise reading the dialogue aloud with your partner.

Connected speech

Weak form of *of*

1 Find a word in the box to complete the phrases below.

| aspirin | sugar | matches | cake |
| cigarettes | tea | water | |

a piece of **cake**

a packet of _____

a cup of _____

a glass of _____

a box of _____

a bottle of _____

a bag of _____

▶▶ p61

2 Look at the stress in these phrases.

☐ ■ ☐ ■
a piece of cake   a packet of cigarettes

T9.5 Listen. *a* and *of* are weak. *of* links with the word before when we speak fast.

/ə/ /əv/   /ə/   /əv/
a piece‿of cake   a packet‿of cigarettes

Practise saying the phrases in 1, paying attention to the stress, weak forms, and linking.

3 **T9.6** Listen and count the words you hear. (*I'd* = two words).

1 [7] _____ like
       _____ wine?

2 ☐ Can _____
       _____ coffee, please?

3 ☐ _____
       bottle _____ aspirin, _____.

4 ☐ _____ packet _____
       _____ box
       _____, please.

Unit 9   37

5 ☐ Daddy, _____ glass _____ ?

6 ☐ _____ potatoes, please.

7 ☐ _____ like _____ ?

▶▶ p61

4 Listen again and write in the missing words.

▶▶ p61

Practise saying the sentences, paying attention to the stress, weak forms, and linking.

5 Work with a partner. Invent a short dialogue to include each of the sentences above.

Would you like a glass of wine?
Oh yes, please.
Red or white?
White, please.

Stress and intonation

Special stress

1 **T9.7** Walter is a waiter in a busy snack bar. Listen to some of his conversations with the customers.

1 **W** So that's two coffees, a beef sandwich, and a tomato soup …
   C *No, a chicken sandwich.*
   W Sorry, sir …

2 **W** Yes, sir?
   C A small mushroom pizza, please.
   W Okay …
   C *No, make that a large mushroom pizza.*
   W Certainly, sir …

3 **W** Okay, so you want one coffee, six colas, four strawberry ice-creams, two chocolate ice-creams, and a piece of apple pie …
   C *No, four chocolate ice-creams and two strawberry …*
   W Anything else?

2 Listen again and look at the lines *in italics*. Underline the words that are specially stressed. Why are these words stressed?

▶▶ p61

38   Unit 9

3 **T9.8** We often use stress and intonation to correct. The intonation goes up and comes down strongly on the word that we want to correct.

No, a <u>chicken</u> sandwich.

Make that a <u>large</u> mushroom pizza.

No, four <u>choc</u>olate ice-creams and two <u>straw</u>berry ...

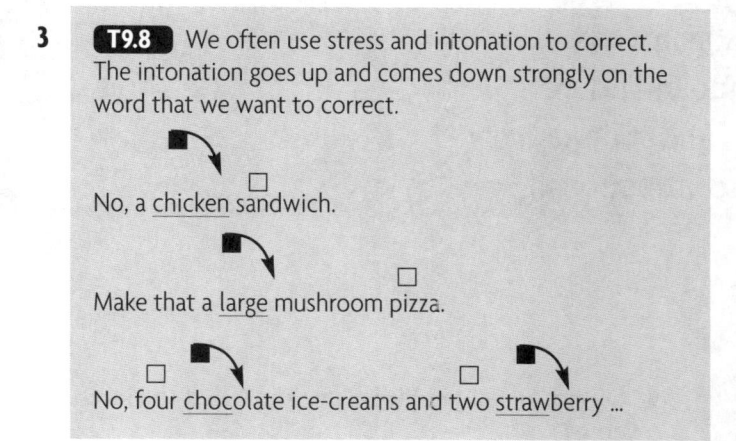

Practise the stress and intonation in these lines.

4 Work with a partner. Practise the four dialogues, putting in the 'special' stress.

5 You and your partner are a waiter and a customer. The waiter makes a lot of mistakes, so the customer corrects him. Use the food on the cards below.

```
WAITER
a beef sandwich
tomato soup
three side salads
a large cheeseburger
two cups of tea and one cup of coffee
```

```
CUSTOMER
a tuna sandwich
chicken soup
two side salads
a small baconburger
two cups of coffee and one cup of tea
```

A: So you want a beef sandwich?

B: No, I want a tuna sandwich!

Remember to stress the words that you want to correct.

Polite requests

We use *Could* to make polite requests.

Could you pass the salt?

Could I use the phone?

But in English, intonation is also very important if you want to sound polite.

1 **T9.9** Listen. All the students in the class want to ask the teacher something – but three of them don't sound polite. Cross (✗) the ones that don't sound polite. Why don't they sound polite?

1 Could you lend me a pen, please?
2 Could you say that again, please?
3 Could you write it on the board, please?
4 Could I open the window, please?
5 Could you help me with this, please?
6 Could you come here, please?

▶▶ p61

2 To sound polite, intonation must not be flat.

Could I open the window, please? ✗

Could I open the window, please? ✓

Start higher up. Practise by humming, like this.

mm mm mm-mm mm MM-mm mm

Could I open the window, please?

T9.10 Listen and practise the requests with polite intonation.

3 Choose four of the requests above that you think will be useful in your English lesson. You have three minutes to remember them. Practise the polite intonation.

4 Now make the requests to your teacher. He/She will only respond if you sound polite!

10

Problem consonants: /h/
Stress in compound nouns
Comparatives and superlatives
Short forms (contractions)

Sounds

Problem consonants: /h/

1 **T10.1** Listen to the pairs of words below. Can you hear the difference?

1	I	(high)	4	ate	hate
2	eat	heat	5	ill	hill
3	air	hair	6	earring	hearing

2 **T10.2** Listen to the sentences and circle the word you hear.

▶▶ p61

3 ◀ **T10.1** Listen again and practise saying the pairs of words.

4 **T10.3** Listen to this dialogue. Check the meaning of new words in your dictionary or with your teacher.

M Who's that with Henry Higgins?
W It's his wife, Hazel.
M Hazel? But his wife's name's Helen!
W Oh no, Helen left him … he's married to Hazel now.
M No! How did it happen?
W Well, you know last Easter, Henry and Helen had a holiday in Honolulu.
M Yes … what happened?
W They had a horrible holiday, and when they arrived home, Helen left him!
M I see … and who are those horrid little girls?
W Holly and Hannah, Hazel's children from her first marriage.
M But Henry *hates* children!
W Mm … how interesting!

5 Work with a partner. Ask and answer these questions.
 1 Who was Henry's first wife?
 2 Who is Henry's second wife?
 3 Are Hannah and Holly …
   … Helen's children?
   … Hazel's children?
   … Henry's children?
 4 Does Henry like children?

▶▶ p61

6 Practise saying the dialogue line by line, pronouncing /h/ correctly. Then practise the dialogue with a partner.

Word focus

Stress in compound nouns

> Many words in English are made by putting two words together. These are called compound nouns.
>
> post + office = post office

1 Take a word from **A** and a word from **B** and put them together to match a picture in column **C**.

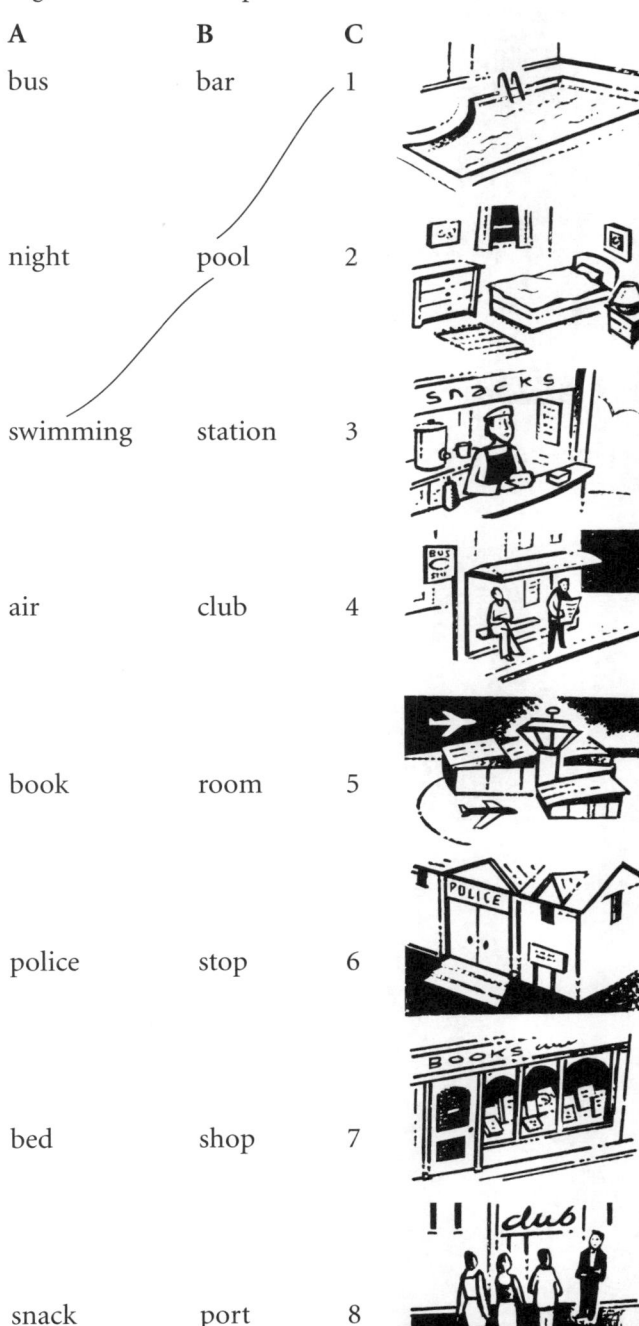

A	B	C
bus	bar	1
night	pool	2
swimming	station	3
air	club	4
book	room	5
police	stop	6
bed	shop	7
snack	port	8

T10.4 Listen and check. Listen again to the word stress. Is it on the first word or the second word?

▶▶ p61

2 **T10.5** Listen and practise saying the compound nouns below. Pay attention to the stress.

living room	hairdresser's	swimming pool
underground station	shoe shop	concert hall
airport	dining room	clothes shop
bathroom	night club	bus stop
leisure centre	wine bar	football stadium

3 Work in groups. Cover the words in 2. Can you remember:

1 Three places to go out in the evening?
2 Three places to travel from?
3 Three places where people do sport?
4 Three rooms in a house?
5 Three shops?

Which group remembered the most words?

▶▶ p61

Connected speech

Comparatives and superlatives

1 Look at the questions below. Do you know the answers?

> **English-speaking countries**
>
> 1 In area, which is the largest country – Australia, Canada, or the USA?
>
> 2 Which is the smaller country in area – New Zealand or the UK?
>
> 3 Which country has the smallest population?
>
> 4 London is the biggest city in the UK. Which is the second biggest – Birmingham or Liverpool?
>
> 5 Which is the oldest city – New York, Washington, or Los Angeles?
>
> 6 Which has the larger population – London or Los Angeles?
>
> 7 Which has the larger population – New York or New Zealand?

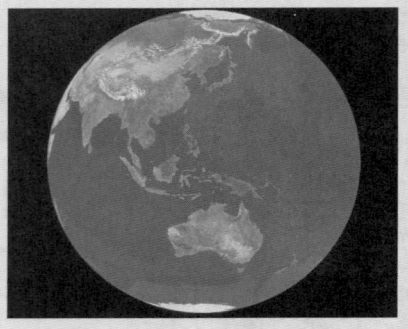

2 **T10.6** Listen and find the answers to the questions.

▶▶ p61

3 **T10.7** Listen to the pronunciation of the comparative and superlative forms of adjectives.

bigger	biggest
higher	highest
larger	largest
older	oldest
smaller	smallest

Look at the comparative and superlative forms in sentences.

☐ ☐ /ə/ /ə/ ■
New York is bigger than Washington.

☐ /ə/ /ɪ/ ☐ ☐ ■
New York is the biggest city in the United States.

than and *the* are weak. They have the vowel sound /ə/.

4 ◀ **T10.6** Look at the tapescript on page 61 and listen to the sentences again. Practise saying them, pronouncing the comparatives and superlatives correctly.

5 Look at the chart below. Make more sentences about these countries.

> Wellington is the smallest city.

> In population, the UK is bigger than Australia.

Country	Area	Population	Cities	
Australia	7.7 m. sq.km.	17 m.	Canberra Sydney	(303,000) (3.2 m.)
Canada	9.9 m. sq.km.	25 m.	Ottawa Montreal	(819,000) (980,000)
New Zealand	269,000 sq.km.	3 m.	Wellington Auckland	(325,000) (144,000)
United Kingdom	244,000 sq.km.	56 m.	London Birmingham Liverpool	(6.4 m.) (920,000) (510,000)
United States	9.4 m. sq.km.	249 m.	Washington New York Los Angeles	(607,000) (7 m.) (2.9 m.)

m. = million   sq.km. = square kilometres

6 Answer the questions below about **your** country/city. Use full sentences, and pronounce the comparatives and superlatives correctly.
1 Is your city bigger or smaller than Auckland?
2 Is it bigger or smaller than Liverpool?
3 In population, is your country larger or smaller than the UK?
4 Is it larger or smaller than Australia, in population?
5 In area, is your country larger or smaller than the UK?
6 Which is the biggest city in your country?
7 Which is the longest river?
8 Which is the highest mountain?
9 Which is the nicest part, do you think?

Short forms (contractions)

1 Look at the sentences below. They are all wrong – why?
1 I got two children.
2 I have a coffee, please.
3 She nineteen years old.
4 I very hungry.
5 I like two Cokes, please.
6 They over there.
7 No, they aren't Spanish – they from Argentina.
8 He got a headache.

Write in the missing short forms, like this.

I ⟨'ve⟩ got two children.

T10.8 Listen and check your answers.

▶▶ p62

2 **T10.9** You will hear some foreign students saying the sentences. Three of them are wrong because the contraction is not pronounced. Listen and tick (✓) the box if the contraction is pronounced, and cross (✗) the box if it is not pronounced.

1 ☐   5 ☐
2 ☐   6 ☐
3 ☐   7 ☐
4 ☐   8 ☐

▶▶ p62

3 ◀ **T10.8** Listen to the correct forms again and practise saying them. Pay attention to the pronunciation of the short forms.

Unit 10   43

11

Introduction to diphthongs
Problem consonants: /n/ and /ŋ/
Word stress (revision)

Sounds

Introduction to diphthongs

> **T11.1** A diphthong is two vowel sounds put together.
>
> **Example** /e/ + /ɪ/ = /eɪ/
>
> The first vowel sound is longer than the second.
> There are eight diphthongs in English.

1 Here are the eight diphthong sounds. Look at the phonemic symbols. Can you guess what the sound is? What is the word in phonemic script?

☐ /eɪ/	/deɪ/	**day**
☐ /aɪ/	/naɪn/	_____
☐ /ɔɪ/	/bɔɪ/	_____
☐ /aʊ/	/naʊ/	_____
☐ /əʊ/	/nəʊ/	_____
☐ /eə/	/heə/	_____
☐ /ɪə/	/hɪə/	_____
☐ /ʊə/*	/tʊə/	_____

T11.2 Listen and tick (✓) the sounds you guessed correctly. Write in the other words.

▶▶ p62

* Many native speakers do not use this diphthong. They use /ɔ:/ instead.

2 Cover the words. Can you remember the words for the sounds? Work with a partner. Test your partner by pointing to the symbols.

3 Read the phonemic symbols and match the phrase to the picture.

1 ə rɪəl bɪəd __g__
2 ə leɪzi deɪ ____
3 feə heə ____
4 nɔɪzi bɔɪz ____
5 ə kəʊld nəʊz ____
6 ə braɪt laɪt ____
7 ə laʊd ʃaʊt ____

a e
b f
c g
d

T11.3 Listen and check your answers.

▶▶ p62

Practise saying the phrases.

4 Look at the phonemic symbols on page 57. Find the words from the box for symbols 37–44. Write them in the spaces under the symbols.

Problem consonants: /n/ and /ŋ/

1 Look at the pairs of words in the square below. Do you understand the meaning from the pictures? Check the meaning of new words in your dictionary or with your teacher.

T11.4 Listen. Can you hear the difference?

1 fans	2 fangs	3 ran	4 rang
5 son	6 sung	7 ban	8 bang
9 Ron	10 wrong	11 win	12 wing
13 thin	14 thing	15 ton	16 tongue

2 Practise the two sounds. To make /n/ and /ŋ/, the air comes out through your nose. Your tongue is further back in your mouth when you make /ŋ/.

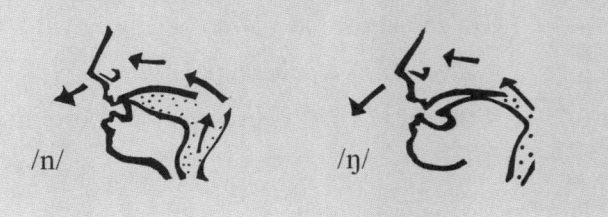

Listen again and practise saying the pairs of words.

3 **T11.5** Listen and circle. Are the sentences true or false?

1. (true) false
2. true false
3. true false
4. true false
5. true false
6. true false

▶▶ p62

Unit 11 45

4 Work with a partner. Make some statements about the pictures on p45 yourself. Your partner will say if they are true or false.

5 Look at the phonemic symbols on page 57. Find the word from the box for sound 24. Write it in the space under the symbol.

Word focus

Word stress (revision)

1 Can you remember the words below? Look at the stress. Which one is correct in British English? Cross out the incorrectly stressed words.

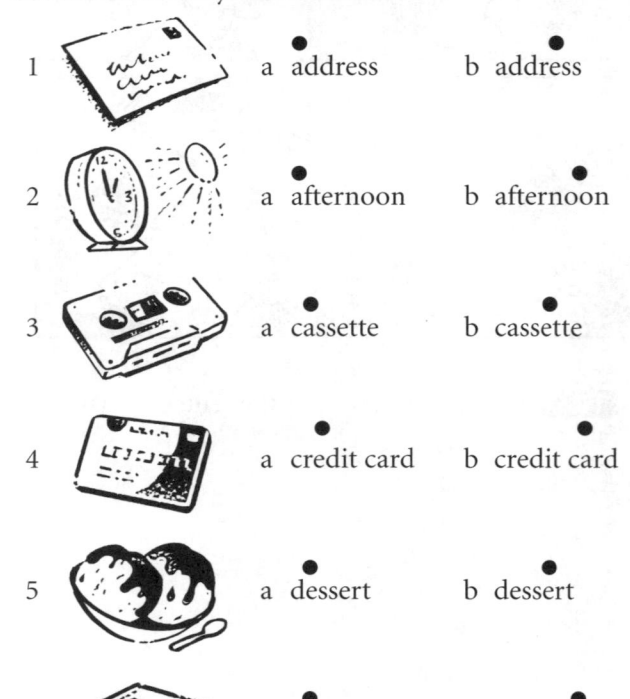

1   a address   b address
2   a afternoon   b afternoon
3   a cassette   b cassette
4   a credit card   b credit card
5   a dessert   b dessert
6   a dictionary   b dictionary
7   a hotel   b hotel
8   a Japan   b Japan
9   a photographer   b photographer
10   a policeman   b policeman
11   a post office   b post office
12   a vegetable   b vegetable

T11.6 Listen and check. How many did you guess correctly?

▶▶ p62

2 Listen again and write the /ə/ sounds in the correct words, like this.

/ə/ •
address

▶▶ p62

Practise saying the words.

3 **T11.7** Listen to some foreign students using the words. Tick (✓) the box if the stress on the word is correct. Cross (✗) the box if it is wrong.

1 ☐ Have you got a *dictionary*?
2 ☐ Do you want any more *vegetables*?
3 ☐ Could I borrow this *cassette*?
4 ☐ Do you know the *address* of your hotel?
5 ☐ My brother's a *policeman*.
6 ☐ I think I left my *credit card* in the post office.

▶▶ p62

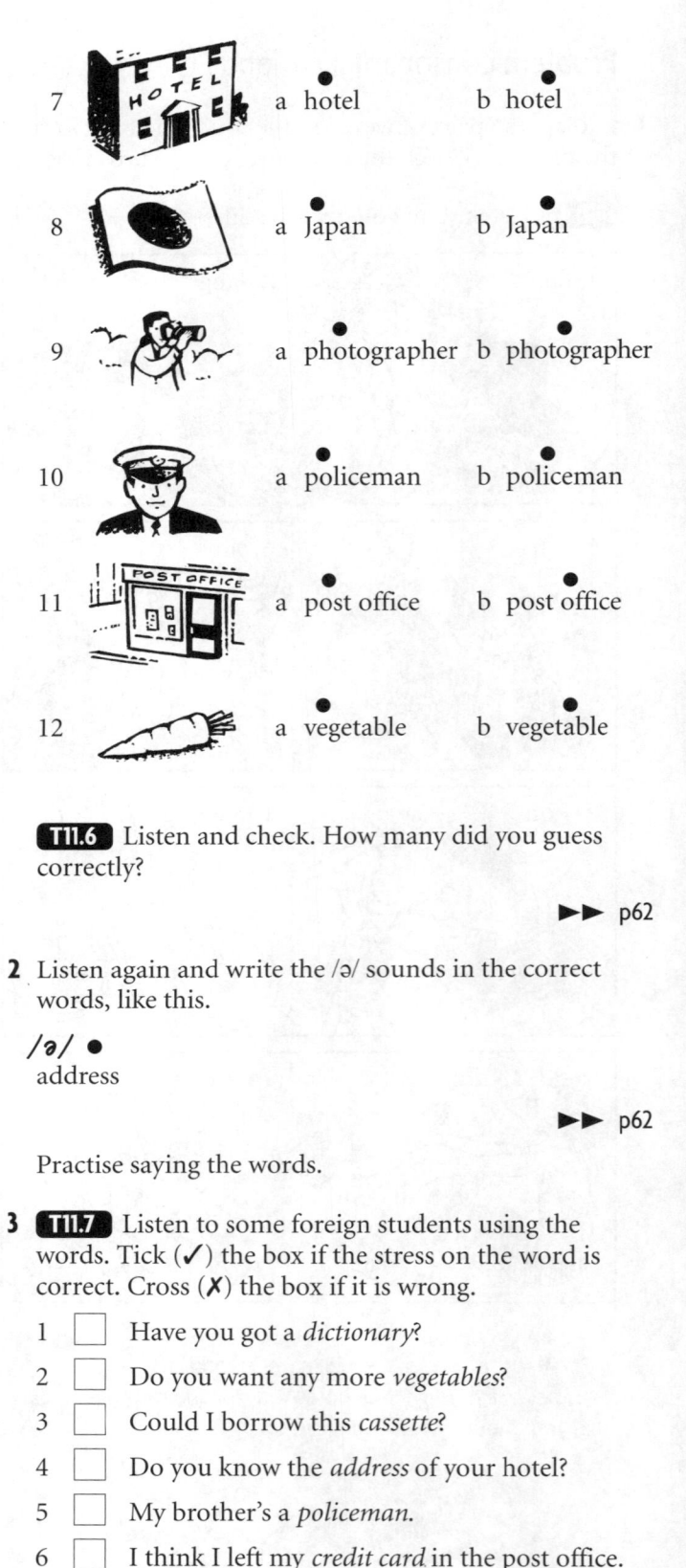

Practise saying the sentences correctly.

12

Problem vowel and diphthong sounds: /ɒ/, /ɔː/, and /əʊ/
Words ending in the sound /ə/
Weak form of *to*
Sounding enthusiastic

Sounds

Problem vowel and diphthong sounds: /ɒ/, /ɔː/, and /əʊ/

1 **T12.1** Listen to the three sounds. Can you hear the difference?

/dʒɒn/ /dʒɔːdʒ/ /dʒəʊ/
John George Jo

Practise saying the three names.

2 **T12.2** Listen and answer the questions about John, George, and Jo. (The sounds /ɒ/, /ɔː/, and /əʊ/ will help you!)

Who …

… is from D**o**ver?	John	George	<u>Jo</u>
… is from B**o**ston?	John	George	Jo
… was b**or**n in Y**or**k?	John	George	Jo
… drinks w**a**ter?	John	George	Jo
… drinks C**o**ca-C**o**la?	John	George	Jo
…drinks c**o**ffee?	John	George	Jo
… plays p**o**lo?	John	George	Jo
… likes g**o**lf and h**o**ckey?	John	George	Jo
… likes **a**ll sp**or**ts?	John	George	Jo
… sm**o**kes a lot?	John	George	Jo
… t**a**lks a lot?	John	George	Jo
… eats a l**o**t of ch**o**colate?	John	George	Jo

▶▶ p62

3 Work with a partner. Ask each other questions, like this.

Sounds and spelling

Words ending in the sound /ə/

1 Look at the words in the box. How is the last syllable pronounced in each word?

camera	answer	picture
mirror	sister	opera
centre	colour	flavour
actor	jumper	hamburger
tuna	signature	departure

T12.3 Listen and practise saying the words.

Unit 12　47

2 Put the words in 1 into the columns below according to their spelling.

1 -er	2 -or	3 -a

4 -ure	5 -re	6 -our

3 Work in groups. Find:

10 more words to go in Column 1.

3 more words to go in Column 2.

3 more words to go in Column 3.

1 more word to go in Columns 4, 5, and 6.

The first group to finish shouts *Stop!*

4 Practise saying your words. Pay attention to the /ə/ sound at the end.

Connected speech

Weak form of *to*

1 Match the parts in **A** and **B** below to make full sentences.

A	B
1 I'm going out	a to see the manager.
2 They're waiting	b to buy a newspaper.
3 My daughter's studying	c to go out with her boyfriend.
4 My brother's going abroad	d to meet some friends.
5 We're going to the airport	e to work.
6 She's getting ready	f to become a doctor.

T12.4 Listen and check your answers.

▶▶ p62

2 Listen again. Note the pronunciation of *to* at the beginning of **B**. Is it strong or weak?

▶▶ p62

3 Practise saying the sentences pronouncing *to* correctly. Start with *to* like this.

/təbaɪ/
to buy … to buy … to buy

to buy a newspaper

out to buy a newspaper

I'm going out to buy a newspaper

Practise saying the other sentences in the same way.

4 **T12.5** The weak *to* is used in other contexts. Listen to the dialogue below and write in the missing *to*s as in the example. There are six more.

D Where are you going, Dad?

F ⟨To⟩ the station meet Mum.

D Oh, what time's her train?

F Twenty five. Do you want come?

D No, I've got go the doctor's at quarter five.

F Oh, yes, well, see you later!

D See you!

▶▶ p62

5 Listen again and practise the dialogue line by line. Pay attention to the pronunciation of *to*. Read the dialogue aloud with a partner.

48   Unit 12

Intonation

Sounding enthusiastic

1 **T12.6** Listen to these conversations at a party. Fill in the gaps in the suggestions below.

1A Let's _____!
1B Okay then!

2A Shall we go into the _____?
2B Okay.

3A Let's have another _____!
3B Okay!

4A Come on, Susie, let's _____ _____!
4B Okay, just a minute.

5A Shall we have a _____ soon?
5B Okay, if you want to.

6A Shall we start the _____ _____?
6B Okay, if you want to.

▶▶ p62

2 B always answers *Okay*, but does B really want to do what A suggests? Listen again and tick (✓) if B really **is** enthusiastic about the suggestion, and cross (✗) the dialogues where B isn't really enthusiastic.

1 ✓   3 ☐   5 ☐
2 ☐   4 ☐   6 ☐

▶▶ p62

3 In the dialogues where B is not enthusiastic, the voice starts low.

Okay

To show enthusiasm, the voice starts high and goes down and then up again, like this.

Okay

Listen again and repeat what B says. Copy the intonation. Practise the dialogues with a partner.

4 Your teacher* will make some suggestions to you. You must always answer *Okay*. Use intonation to show if you're really enthusiastic.

5 Make a suggestion yourself. See how the class responds!

* See the Answer key on page 62.

Unit 12   49

13

Problem vowel and diphthong sounds: /e/ and /eɪ/
Problem consonants: /ʃ/ and /tʃ/
The sound /ə/ in final syllables
Linking (revision)

Sounds

Problem vowel and diphthong sounds: /e/ and /eɪ/

1 **T13.1** Listen to the pairs of words below. Can you hear the difference?

   pen   pain
   tell   tail
   wet   wait

2 Now look at these words. Check the meaning of new words in your dictionary or with your teacher.

   T13.2 Listen and circle the word you hear.

   1 men   main
   2 let   late
   3 get   gate
   4 sell   sail

   ▶▶ p62

3 You make the sound /e/ at the front of your mouth. Your lips look like this.

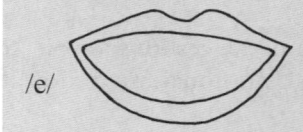

   /e/

   To make the sound /eɪ/, first make a long /e/ sound and then a short /ɪ/ sound.

   /e/ → /ɪ/

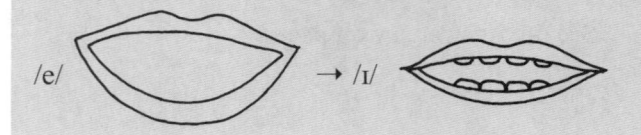

   Now practise saying the pairs of words in 1.

4 **T13.3** Listen to Jenny talking about her holiday. Are the **bold** sounds /e/ or /eɪ/? Mark the /e/ sounds like this ___ and the /eɪ/ sounds like this ～.

   Last year, I w**e**nt to Sp**ai**n on holid**ay** with my fri**e**nd J**a**ne. The hot**e**l was gr**ea**t, but the w**ea**ther was t**e**rrible! It r**ai**ned **e**very d**ay** for t**e**n d**ay**s!

   ▶▶ p62

5 How many examples of /e/ and /eɪ/ can you find in these sentences? Mark them in the same way as 4.

   1 An African elephant weighs five to seven tonnes.
   2 Elvis Presley played rock 'n' roll.
   3 The train from Newcastle to London takes four hours.
   4 We met in the USA in 1986.
   5 Julie read about the weather in Budapest.

   T13.4 Listen and check your answers.

   ▶▶ p62

6 Practise reading the sentences in 5. Pay attention to the /e/ and /eɪ/ sounds.

Problem consonants: /ʃ/ and /tʃ/

1 **T13.5** Listen to these words.

| shirt | sugar | delicious | dishwasher | pronunciation |

The sound /ʃ/ is often spelt *sh*. What other ways is it spelt?

▶▶ p62

2 Look at the text about Sheila. How many examples of the /ʃ/ sound can you hear? Underline them.

Sheila is a receptionist at the International Hotel in Chicago. At the moment she's studying Spanish.

T13.6 Listen and check your answers.

▶▶ p62

3 To make the sound /ʃ/, first practise /s/. Now move your tongue back and up a little. It is the sound we make when we want people to be quiet!

Practise reading the text about Sheila aloud, paying attention to the /ʃ/ sound.

4 **T13.7** Listen. Can you hear the difference?

| she's | cheese | sheep | cheap |
| shoes | choose | wash | watch |

The second word in each pair has the sound /tʃ/. To make the sound /tʃ/, first say /t/. Then say /ʃ/. Repeat each sound quickly until you say the two sounds together. The sound /tʃ/ is usually spelt *ch*.

5 Look at the picture below. Can you find:

a Spanish beach?   Sheila catching a fish?
some Scottish children?   an English teacher?
a Frenchman eating cheese? a pair of cheap shoes?
two Chinese men playing chess?

T13.8 Listen to the phrases. Underline the sound /ʃ/ like this ___ and the sound /tʃ/ like this ∿.

▶▶ p63

6 Practise saying the words. Work with a partner, like this.

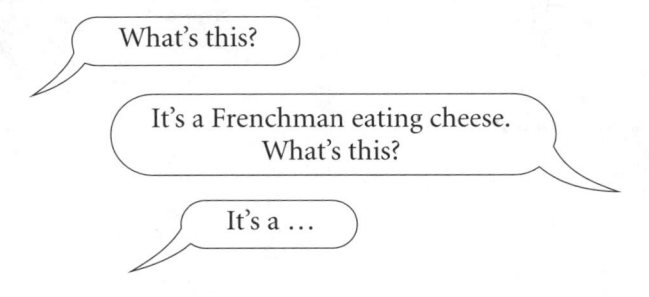

> What's this?
>
> It's a Frenchman eating cheese. What's this?
>
> It's a …

7 Look at the phonemic symbols on page 57. Find the words from the box for sounds 20 and 22. Write them in the spaces under the symbols.

Unit 13 51

Sounds and spelling

The sound /ə/ in final syllables

1 Write in the missing letters.

1 Americ_**a**_n
   German   _Mexican_

2 seas___n
   _____   _____

3 childr___n
   _____   _____

4 music___n
   _____   _____

5 televis___n
   _____   _____

6 conversat___n
   _____   _____

7 beautif___l
   _____   _____

8 nation___l
   _____   _____

9 intellig___nt
   _____   _____

10 nerv___s
   _____   _____

▶▶ p63

2 The final syllable in the words in 1 is spelt differently in each word, but the vowel sound in the final syllable is always /ə/.

| /ə/ | /ə/ | /ə/ | /ə/ |
| American | season | children | musician |

T13.9 Listen and practise saying the words in 1. Pay attention to the sound /ə/ in the final syllables.

3 Look at the box below and find **two** words with the same ending as each word in 1. Write them in the spaces.

German	successful	London	decision
listen	station	optician	revision
arrival	parent	careful	pardon
Mexican	garden	student	famous
delicious	hospital	beautician	pronunciation

T13.10 Listen and check your answers.

▶▶ p63

4 Practise saying the words. Can you think of any more words to put in each group?

5 Think of phrases with these words.

Examples
a successful student
a famous garden
a German hospital

Practise saying the phrases.

52 Unit 13

Connected speech

Linking (revision)

1 Look at the words below. Check the meaning of new words in your dictionary or with your teacher.

absolutely	ambulance	attractive
awful	excellent	experience
immediately	incredible	area

2 **T13.11** You will hear some sentences. If they have an adjective, write *adj*; if they have an adverb, write *adv*; and if they have an adjective and an adverb, write *both*.

1 _____adj_____ 5 _____
2 _____ 6 _____
3 _____ 7 _____
4 _____ 8 _____

▶▶ p63

3 Listen again and fill in the gaps in the sentences.

1 What a _____ _____ !

2 It was an _____ _____ .

3 The weather was _____ _____ !

4 He got into their _____ _____ .

5 She speaks _____ _____ and _____ .

6 It was an _____ _____ !

7 She lives in a _____ _____ .

8 I'll phone for an _____ _____ !

▶▶ p63

4 Notice the linking between words **A** and **B**.

| A | B | A | B |
| What_a | | fantastic_idea | |

What kind of sound does **A** end with? What kind of sound does **B** begin with?

▶▶ p63

5 Look at the other sentences in 3 and mark the linking.

▶▶ p63

Listen again and practise putting in the linking.

Unit 13 53

14

Problem consonants: /tʃ/, /dʒ/, and /j/
Words with similar vowel sounds
Contractions and weak forms in the Present Perfect

Sounds

Problem consonants: /tʃ/, /dʒ/, and /j/

1 **T14.1** Listen to the words below. Can you hear the difference between the three consonant sounds?

/tʃ/ — Chess   /dʒ/ — Jess   /j/ — Yes

2 Say the three words. Which ones are most difficult for you? Practise saying these again.

> To make /j/ first start with the sound /iː/.
>
>   i i i ... yes
>   i i ... yes
>   i ... yes
>
> You practised /dʒ/ in Unit 8, and /tʃ/ in Unit 13. Remember that you use your voice for /dʒ/ but you do not use your voice for /tʃ/.

3 **T14.2** The words below are similar in many languages. In English they all begin with one of the sounds above: /tʃ/, /dʒ/ or /j/. Listen and write the correct symbol in the box.

1. [tʃ] chocolate
2. [ ] yoga
3. [ ] chimpanzee
4. [ ] yacht
5. [ ] jacket
6. [ ] chess
7. [ ] yoghurt

54   Unit 14

8 ☐ gin

9 ☐ geography

10 ☐ jeans

▶▶ p63

4 Complete the rule with the correct phonemic symbols. Add an example from the words in 3.

Spelling rule

1 The letter *y* (at the beginning of a word) is pronounced / /.

   Example _____

2 a The letter *j* is pronounced / /.

   Example _____

   b The letters *ge* and *gi* are often pronounced / /.

   Examples _____ , _____

3 The letters *ch* are often pronounced / /.

   Example _____

   There are some exceptions, however.
   ch = /k/ in *chemist*, *character*, *Christmas*.
   ch = /ʃ/ in *chef*, *champagne*.
   ch = not pronounced in *yacht*.

▶▶ p63

5 Practise saying the words in 3 above. Remember the rules.

6 Look at the phonemic symbols on page 57. Find the word from the box for sound 17. Write it in the space under the symbol.

Words with similar vowel sounds

1 The pairs of words below are easy to confuse. Do you remember what they all mean? Tick (✓) the ones you're sure you can pronounce correctly. Put a question mark (?) next to the ones you're not sure about.

☐ angry ☐ hungry
☐ leave ☐ live
☐ this ☐ these
☐ where ☐ were
☐ want ☐ won't
☐ walk ☐ work

T14.3 Listen and check. Practise saying the pairs of words.

2 **T14.4** Now listen to the conversation and put the words into the correct box below.

1	2	3	4
5	6	7	8
9	10	11	12

▶▶ p63

3 Play the game with a partner. Your partner must tell you where to write the words.

1	2	3	4
5	6	7	8
9	10	11	12

Unit 14   55

Connected speech

Contractions and weak forms in the Present Perfect

1 **T14.5** Listen to the sentences below. You will hear each one twice. One time *have/has/haven't/hasn't* is pronounced correctly. The other time it is pronounced incorrectly. Which is correct? Tick **a** or **b**.

1 I've never seen it.   a ✓   b ☐
2 She's just come back.   a ☐   b ☐
3 He hasn't phoned yet.   a ☐   b ☐
4 We haven't been here.   a ☐   b ☐
5 Has your sister gone out?   a ☐   b ☐
6 Yes, she has.   a ☐   b ☐
7 Have you been to the shops?   a ☐   b ☐
8 Yes, I have.   a ☐   b ☐

▶▶ p63

Notice the pronunciation of the contractions.

I've = /aɪv/   haven't = /hævənt/
He's = /hiːz/   hasn't = /hæzənt/

In questions, the weak form is used.

/həv/
Have you been to the shops?

/həz/
Has your sister gone out?

In short answers *have* and *has* are strong.

/hæv/   /hæz/
Yes, I have.   Yes, she has.

---

2 **T14.6** Listen now to the correct sentences only and practise the pronunciation of *have/haven't*, etc.

3 **T14.7** Listen to a dialogue between two neighbours. They are talking about holidays in Italy. Look at the words below. Underline the things that they talk about.

pasta	gondolas	the Pope
the beaches	the Colosseum	Italian clothes
Pompeii	the Leaning Tower of Pisa	

4 Listen again.
1 How many times do you hear *have* or *has*?
2 How many times do you hear *'ve* or *'s*?
3 How many times do you hear *haven't* or *hasn't*?

Put a tick (✓) in the correct box below each time you hear these forms.

have or has	
've or 's	
haven't or hasn't	

▶▶ p63

5 Work with a partner. Look at the tapescript of the dialogue on page 63 and practise it with a partner. Pay attention to the pronunciation of the different forms of *have*.

6 Read the secret message.

ðɪs ɪz ə siːkrɪt mesɪdʒ

ɪf juː nəʊ ɔːl ðə fəniːmɪk sɪmbəlz juː dəʊnt niːd tə stʌdi peɪdʒ fɪfti-sevən əgen.

▶▶ p63

Phonemic symbols

Consonants

1 /p/	2 /b/	3 /t/	4 /d/	5 /k/	6 /g/	7 /f/	8 /v/

9 /s/	10 /z/	11 /l/	12 /m/	13 /n/	14 /h/	15 /r/	16 /w/

17 /j/	18 /θ/	19 /ð/	20 /ʃ/	21 /ʒ/	22 /tʃ/	23 /dʒ/	24 /ŋ/
				television			

Vowels

25 /i:/	26 /ɪ/	27 /e/	28 /æ/	29 /ɑ:/	30 /ɒ/	31 /ɔ:/	32 /ʊ/

33 /u:/	34 /ʌ/	35 /ɜ:/	36 /ə/

Diphthongs

37 /eɪ/	38 /əʊ/	39 /aɪ/	40 /aʊ/	41 /ɔɪ/	42 /ɪə/	43 /eə/	44 /ʊə/

Look at the sound underlined in the words below.
Put the words under the correct symbol for that sound.

man	why	that	ticket	start	choose	jeans	sing	yellow
television	tea	pencil	bag	shoe	is	like	read	we
hair	good	lives	bed	five	do	sit	three	door
sister	vocabulary	hand	go	key	not	your	love	Greece
girl	day	no	down	hot	noise	beer	tour	

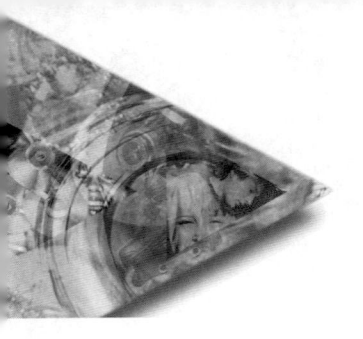

Key

Unit 1

The sound of English

1 1 b 2 a 3 a 4 c 5 a 6 a 7 b 8 c

3
● photograph   ● police   ● radio
● passport   ● toilet   ● email

Stress in numbers

2 b finishes first.
c finishes second.
a finishes third.

T1.7
fifty … fifty
thirteen … thirteen
seventeen … seventeen
thirty … thirty
eighteen … eighteen
fifteen … fifteen
ninety … ninety
sixteen … sixteen
fourteen … fourteen
nineteen … nineteen
eighty … eighty
sixty … sixty
forty … forty
seventy … seventy

Short forms (contractions) of be

2 **T1.8**
Hello. I'm Jane. This is my cat. Her name's Pepper. She's three years old and she's very intelligent, I think!

That's my dog, Sam. Sam's twelve years old now! He's a very nice dog, but he's very stupid!

Unit 2

Introduction to vowel sounds (1)

1 1 /iː/ and /uː/ are long sounds.

2 1 /iː/   5 /iː/   9 /ʊ/
2 /e/   6 /iː/   10 /ɪ/
3 /ɪ/   7 /ɪ/
4 /ɪ/   /ɪ/   8 /iː/

Problem consonants: final '-s'

1 1 cups /s/   3 Anna's /z/ friend
pens /z/   Jane's /z/ bag
stamps /s/   Pete's /s/ mum

2 speaks /s/   4 It's /s/ here.
reads /z/   How's /z/ Andy?
loves /z/   He's /z/ okay.

The sound /ə/

2
● /ə/   ● /ə/ ● /ə/
hamburger   mineral water

● /ə/   ● /ə/ ● /ə/
pizza   Coca-Cola

● /ə/
salads

3 1 c 2 g 3 b 4 e 5 h 6 d 7 i
8 f 9 j 10 a

4 1, 2, 3, 5, 7, and 8 have an /ə/ sound.

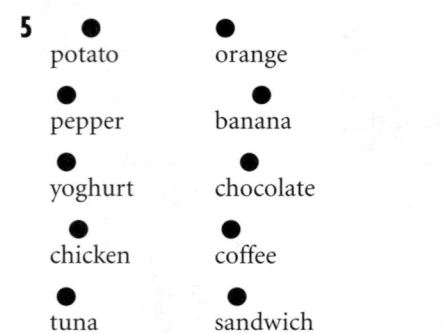

5
● potato   ● orange
● pepper   ● banana
● yoghurt   ● chocolate
● chicken   ● coffee
● tuna   ● sandwich

Introduction to sentence stress

3
□ ■
Where are you from?
□ ■
What's your job?
■ □
How old are you?
□ ■
Are you married?

Unit 3

Silent 'r'

2 inte~~r~~preter   ba~~r~~man
nu~~r~~se   a~~r~~tist
a~~r~~chitect   receptionist
docto~~r~~   write~~r~~
directo~~r~~

3 Examples of words where *r* is pronounced:
drive   from
different   countries
France   very
address   brown
children   friendly
interesting   green
underground   horrible
write

Examples of words where *r* is not pronounced:
October   Dear
are   international
other   they're
Argentina   Switzerland
teacher   Peter
letter   fourteen
underground   understand
weather   parks
centre

58 Key

Weak forms and linking

1 get up – go to bed
open – close
arrive – leave
start – finish

2 1 6   2 7   3 7   4 7   5 6   6 7
7 7   8 7

3 T3.4
1 The bank opens at nine o'clock.
2 He goes to bed at seven o'clock.
3 This office closes at half past two.
4 We get up at about eight o'clock.
5 Her plane arrives at two fifteen.
6 The programme finishes at about eleven thirty.
7 The film starts at half past eight.
8 My train leaves at about eleven o'clock.

6 5 Her plane‿arrives‿at two fifteen.
6 The programme finishes‿at‿about‿eleven thirty.
7 The film starts‿at half past‿eight.
8 My train leaves‿at‿about‿eleven‿o'clock.

Introduction to intonation: up or down?

1 1 statement – question
2 statement – question
3 question – statement
4 question – statement

Unit 4

Weak forms in Present Simple questions

T4.2
1 A Do you know the time?
  B It's quarter past three.
2 A Do you have a light?
  B No, sorry.
3 A Do you speak English?
  B Yes, a little.
4 A Do you understand?
  B Not really.
5 A Do you have milk?
  B Yes, please.
6 A What do you do?
  B I'm a musician.

Weak forms of *a* and *the*

1 T4.4
M Do you have children, Shirley?
S Yes, a son and a daughter.
M Oh, that's nice, what do they do?
S My daughter Jenny's a music teacher, and Michael, my son, is at college – he wants to be a pilot!
M Oh, lovely!
S Yes …
M Do they live at home?
S Michael lives with me, but Jenny lives in London – she's married with two children.
M Oh! So you're a grandmother!
S Yes, she has a girl and a boy too – Rebecca and Thomas.
M Oh, lovely – how old are they?
S The girl's seven and the boy's two – do you want to see a photo?
M Oh yes. … Ah … aren't they beautiful!

How many syllables?

1 **Across:** 2 interesting 3 chocolate
4 restaurant 6 vegetables
9 dictionary 10 February
Down: 1 Wednesday 3 camera
5 married 7 every 8 soldier

2 camera 2   married 2
chocolate 2   restaurant 2
dictionary 3   soldier 2
every 2   vegetables 3
February 3   Wednesday 2
interesting 3

3
● cam(e)ra   ● marri(e)d
● choc(o)late   ● restau(r)ant
● diction(a)ry   ● sold(i)er
● ev(e)ry   ● veg(e)tables
● Febru(a)ry   ● Wedn(e)sday
● int(e)resting

5 1 1 /ɑːnt/   4 3 /kʌmftəbl/
    2 2 /iːvnɪŋ/   5 2 /fæmli/
    3 2 /feɪvrɪt/   6 3 /sekrətri/

Unit 5

Introduction to vowel sounds (2)

3 word – curtain   bus – cup
four – wall   part – carpet
man – lamp   shop – pots

4 T5.3
1 h 2 d 3 b 4 a 5 e 6 g 7 i
8 c 9 f 10 j
a bath   f television
b garden   g mirror
c living room   h fridge
d door   i cooker
e cupboard   j washing machine

Sounding polite

4 T5.7
Desk 1
Hello. Can I help you?
Yes, please. Is the Museum of Modern Art near here?
Mmm, just a minute … here's a map …

Desk 2
Next, please.
Hello, can you help me? I want a hotel for three nights.
Sorry, we don't have information about hotels. Try next door.
Thank you.

Desk 3
Excuse me …
Yes, sir?
Is there a bookshop near here?
Sure, on the left opposite the underground station.

Unit 6

Problem consonants: /w/

1 1 Wendy was twenty-one Wednesday
2 Where was William weekend
3 We want Wayne We want Wayne
4 What wonderful world

4 when 9   winter 4   two 2
week 8   we 1   what 12
wrong 5   swim 10   twenty 7
who 3   whole 11   write 6

5 Words with a silent *w*:
wrong who whole two write

6 a wrong   b whole

Key 59

7 `T6.2`
(You hear the words in 5 above.)

Can and can't

1 `T6.3`
1. **B** I can play football okay.
   I I can play football. I'm really good at it. I'm in the school team!
2. **B** Of course I can use a computer!
   I I can use a computer.
3. **B** I can swim about 400 metres actually!
   I I can't swim 100 metres. I can swim about 25 metres, I think.

4 and 5
   B I can ride a bicycle, but I can't ride a horse.
   I I can't ride a bicycle very well, but I can ride a horse!
6. **B** I can't sew really.
   I I can't sew ... not very well.
7. **B** I can speak French a bit.
   I I can't speak French ... no.
8. **B** I can't play the piano.
   I I can play the piano ... a bit!
9. **B** I can run really fast!
   I I can't run very fast.

	Ben	Isabel
play football	✓	✓
use a computer	✓	✓
swim 100 metres	✓	✗
ride a bicycle	✓	✗
ride a horse	✗	✓
sew	✗	✗
speak French	✓	✗
play the piano	✗	✓
run fast	✓	✗

Pronunciation of negative forms

1
1 ✓   6 ✗   11 ✓
2 ✓   7 ✓   12 ✓
3 ✓   8 ✓   13 ✗
4 ✗   9 ✓
5 ✗   10 ✗

2
1 were   8 Could
2 were   9 could
3 were   10 couldn't
4 weren't   11 Can
5 wasn't   12 can
6 couldn't 13 can't
7 was

Unit 7

Problem vowel sounds /ɪ/ and /i:/

2
1 sit   3 bean   5 heel
2 hit   4 ship   6 lick

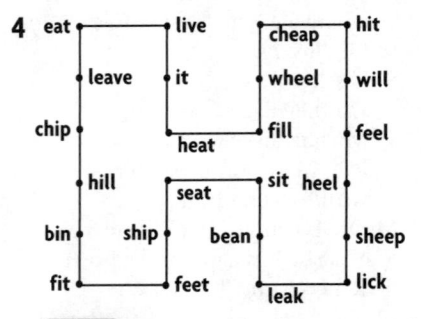

4
eat — live   cheap — hit
leave — it   wheel — will
chip   heat — fill — feel
hill   seat — sit — heel
bin — ship   bean — sheep
fit — feet   leak — lick

`T7.2`
Start at *eat* ... draw a line from *eat* to *live* ... then from *live* to *it* ... from *it* draw a line to *heat* ... and from *heat* to *fill* ... then go from *fill* to *wheel* ... and from *wheel* to *cheap* ... from *cheap* draw a line to *hit* ... then from *hit* go to *will* ... and from *will* to *feel* ... then to *heel* ... then to *sheep* ... and down to *lick* ... okay? Right, now go to *leak* ... then from *leak* to *bean* ... and from *bean* to *sit* ... from *sit* go to *seat* ... and then from *seat* go to *ship* and down to *feet* ... all right? Now from *feet* you go to *fit* ... from *fit* you go up to *bin* ... then *hill* ... then up to *chip* ... then to *leave* ... and then finally back up to *eat* ... what have you got?

Past Simple forms that are difficult to pronounce

1
1 read   6 heard
2 learnt   7 bought
3 ran   8 said
4 fell   9 taught
5 saw   10 thought

3 `T7.3`
(You hear 1–6 as in 1 above.)

4
see – saw   put – put
think – thought   send – sent
catch – caught   pay – paid
read – read   teach – taught
buy – bought   say – said
cut – cut   mean – meant
wear – wore

5 1 ✓ 2 ✓ 3 ✗ 4 ✓ 5 ✓ 6 ✓ 7 ✗

Hearing Past Simple forms

2 /t/   /d/

4 `T7.7`
1 arrived   4 closed
2 opened   5 start
3 finish   6 stopped

Intonation in Wh- questions

2 1 c 2 b 3 c 4 a 5 a 6 c 7 a

`T7.9` `T7.10`
1 *Where were* you born?
  In New York.
2 *When was* your sister born?
  In 1978.
3 *When was* your birthday?
  In March.
4 *When did* her grandfather die?
  Last year.
5 *How old* was he?
  About 80.
6 *Where did you* go to university?
  In London.
7 *When did* you leave university?
  In 1993.

Unit 8

Problem consonants: /dʒ/

2
1 John Lennon
2 Mick Jagger
3 Jackie Kennedy
4 George Clooney
5 Julia Roberts
6 George Michael

Problem vowel sounds: /ɜ:/

1 No. In British English the *r* is not pronounced. In American English it **is** pronounced.

2
Thursday   birthday
person   journey
university   hamburger
Germany   thirtieth
journalist

There is no /ɜ:/ sound in *Saturday*, *restaurant*, and *conversation*.

4
1 ɜ: B<u>ir</u>mingham g<u>ir</u>l m<u>ur</u>dered
2 ɜ: N<u>ur</u>se K<u>ir</u>sty T<u>ur</u>key
3 ɜ: th<u>ir</u>tieth b<u>ir</u>thday
4 ɜ: German university b<u>ur</u>ns
5 ɜ: w<u>or</u>kers w<u>or</u>st w<u>or</u>ld

60 Key

Saying dates

2 ▌T8.5

1 St Valentine's Day is the day of lovers – it's on the fourteenth of February.
2 April Fool's Day, on the first of April, is the day when people play jokes on their friends and families.
3 St George's Day is on the twenty-third of April – St George is the patron saint of England.
4 The Queen has an official birthday on the second of June, but her real birthday is on the twenty-first of April.
5 Halloween is on the thirty-first of October – it's a night when witches are supposed to come out!
6 On Guy Fawkes Night we remember the time when a man called Guy Fawkes tried to destroy the Houses of Parliament. It's on the fifth of November.
7 Remembrance Sunday is the day when we remember all the people who died in the First and Second World Wars. It's always on the second Sunday in November.
8 St Andrew's Day is on the thirtieth of November – St Andrew is the patron saint of Scotland … and Russia!

3 ▌T8.6

/əv/
the fourteenth_of February
/əv/
the first_of_April
/əv/
the twenty-third_of_April
/əv/
the second_of June
/əv/
the twenty-first_of_April
/əv/
the thirty-first_of_October
/əv/
the fifth_of November
/əv/
the thirtieth_of November

Unit 9

Problem vowel sounds: /æ/ and /ʌ/

3 ▌T9.3

Bag 1 /æ/	Bag 2 /ʌ/
jam	bun
apple	onion
cabbage	honey
carrot	mushroom
ham	butter
salad	cucumber

4 1 *a*   2 *u, o*

8 /æ/ ham scrambled salad have jam thanks

/ʌ/ Mum supper much mushroom just butter love none nothing cup lovely

Weak form of *of*

1 a piece of cake
a packet of cigarettes
a cup of tea
a glass of water
a box of matches
a bottle of aspirin
a bag of sugar

3 1 7 2 8 3 8 4 10 5 8 6 5 7 7

4 ▌T9.6

1 Would you like a glass of wine?
2 Can I have a cup of coffee, please?
3 I'd like a bottle of aspirin, please.
4 A packet of cigarettes and a box of matches, please.
5 Daddy, can I have a glass of milk?
6 A bag of potatoes, please.
7 Would you like a piece of cake?

Special stress

2 1 chicken
2 large
3 chocolate strawberry
These words are stressed because the speaker wants to correct a mistake.

Polite requests

1 Students 3, 4, and 6 do not sound polite.

Unit 10

Problem consonants: /h/

2 1 high 2 eat 3 air 4 hate 5 hill
6 earring

▌T10.2

1 It's high!
2 Can you eat this?
3 This air's very dirty.
4 I hate it.
5 Did you say *hill*?
6 She's got a problem with her earring.

5 1 Helen 2 Hazel 3 Hazel's children
4 No

Stress in compound nouns

1 ▌T10.4

1 swimming pool   5 airport
2 bedroom   6 police station
3 snack bar   7 bookshop
4 bus stop   8 night club
The stress is on the first word.

3 1 night club
wine bar
concert hall
2 underground station
airport
bus stop
3 leisure centre
swimming pool
football stadium
4 living room
bathroom
dining room
5 hairdresser's
shoe shop
clothes shop

Comparatives and superlatives

2 ▌T10.6

1 In area, Canada is the largest. The USA is bigger than Australia.
2 The UK is smaller than New Zealand in area.
3 New Zealand has the smallest population.
4 Birmingham is bigger than Liverpool.
5 New York is the oldest.
6 London has a larger population than Los Angeles.

Key 61

7 New York has a larger population than New Zealand.

Short forms (contractions)

1 ▪ T10.8
1 I've got two children.
2 I'll have a coffee, please.
3 She's nineteen years old.
4 I'm very hungry.
5 I'd like two Cokes, please.
6 They're over there.
7 No, they aren't Spanish – they're from Argentina.
8 He's got a headache.

2 1 ✓ 2 ✗ 3 ✓ 4 ✓ 5 ✗ 6 ✓ 7 ✗ 8 ✓

Unit 11

Introduction to diphthongs

1 ▪ T11.2
day   no / know
nine   hair
boy   hear / here
now   tour

3 ▪ T11.3
1 a real beard (g)
2 a lazy day (d)
3 fair hair (b)
4 noisy boys (f)
5 a cold nose (a)
6 a bright light (e)
7 a loud shout (c)

Problem consonants: /n/ and /ŋ/

3 1 true 2 false 3 true 4 false
5 false 6 false

▪ T11.5
1 In number 1, there are a lot of fans.
2 Someone rang in number 3.
3 There's a bang in number 8.
4 The man in number 9 is wrong.
5 Number 14 is 'thin'.
6 There's a tongue in number 15.

Word stress (revision)

1 The **correctly** stressed words are:
1 b   4 a   7 b   10 b
2 b   5 b   8 b   11 a
3 b   6 a   9 b   12 a

2
        /ə/ ●   /ə/ ● /ə/ /ə/
2 afternoon   9 photographer
        /ə/ ●   /ə/ ● /ə/
3 cassette   10 policeman
        ● /ə/   ●   /ə/
6 dictionary   12 vegetable
        /ə/ ●
8 Japan

4, 5, 7, and 11 have no /ə/ sound.

3 1 ✓ 2 ✗ 3 ✗ 4 ✗ 5 ✗ 6 ✓

Unit 12

Problem vowel and diphthong sounds: /ɒ/, /ɔː/, and /əʊ/

2 Dover – Jo
Boston – John
born in York – George
water – George
Coca-Cola – Jo
coffee – John
polo – Jo
golf and hockey – John
all sports – George
smokes – Jo
talks – George
a lot of chocolate – John

▪ T12.2
John John's from Boston. He drinks coffee and plays golf and hockey. He eats a lot of chocolate.
George George is from York. He drinks water and likes all sports. He talks and talks and talks and talks …
Jo Jo comes from Dover. She loves Coca-Cola, and her favourite sport is polo. She smokes a lot.

Words ending in the sound /ə/

1 The last syllable is pronounced /ə/.

2 1 answer, sister, jumper, hamburger
2 mirror, actor
3 camera, tuna, opera
4 signature, picture, departure
5 centre
6 colour, flavour

Weak form of *to*

1 ▪ T12.4
1 I'm going out to buy a newspaper.
2 They're waiting to see the manager.
3 My daughter's studying to become a doctor.
4 My brother's going abroad to work.
5 We're going to the airport to meet some friends.
6 She's getting ready to go out with her boyfriend.

2 weak

4 ▪ T12.5
D Where are you going, Dad?
F To the station to meet Mum.
D Oh, what time's her train?
F Twenty to five. Do you want to come?
D No. I've got to go to the doctor's at quarter to five.
F Oh, yes, well, see you later!
D See you!

Sounding enthusiastic

1 1A dance   4A go home
2A garden   5A party
3A drink   6A washing-up

2 1 ✓ 2 ✗ 3 ✓ 4 ✗ 5 ✓ 6 ✗

4 1 Let's play a game!
2 Shall we do some writing now?
3 Let's have a break!
4 Shall we go out for coffee?
5 Let's have a test next week!
6 Shall we have a class party?

Unit 13

Problem vowel and diphthong sounds: /e/ and /eɪ/

2 ▪ T13.2
1 main 2 let 3 get 4 sail

4 Last year, I w<u>e</u>nt to Sp<u>ai</u>n on holid<u>ay</u> with my fr<u>ie</u>nd J<u>a</u>ne. The hotel was gr<u>ea</u>t, but the w<u>ea</u>ther was t<u>e</u>rrible! It r<u>ai</u>ned <u>e</u>very d<u>ay</u> for t<u>e</u>n days!

5 1 An African <u>e</u>lephant w<u>ei</u>ghs five to s<u>e</u>ven tonnes.
2 Elvis Pr<u>e</u>sley pl<u>ay</u>ed rock 'n' roll.
3 The tr<u>ai</u>n from Newcastle to London t<u>a</u>kes four hours.
4 We m<u>e</u>t in the US<u>A</u> in 19<u>8</u>6.
5 Julie r<u>ea</u>d about the w<u>ea</u>ther in Budap<u>e</u>st.

Problem consonants: /ʃ/ and /tʃ/

1 /ʃ/ is also spelt *s*, *ci*, and *ti* in the examples.

2 6
Sheila is a receptionist at the International Hotel in Chicago. At the moment she's studying Spanish.

5 a Spanish beach
some Scottish children
a Frenchman eating cheese
two Chinese men playing chess
Sheila catching a fish
an English teacher
a pair of cheap shoes

The sound /ə/ in final syllables

1 1 *a*   4 *ia*   7 *u*   10 *ou*
2 *o*   5 *io*   8 *a*
3 *e*   6 *io*   9 *e*

3
1	German	Mexican
2	London	pardon
3	listen	garden
4	optician	beautician
5	decision	revision
6	station	pronunciation
7	successful	careful
8	arrival	hospital
9	parent	student
10	delicious	famous

Linking (revision)

2 1 adj   3 both   5 adj   7 both
2 adj   4 adv   6 adj   8 adv

3 ▶ T13.11
1 What a fantastic idea!
2 It was an easy exam.
3 The weather was absolutely awful!
4 He got into their office easily.
5 She speaks excellent English and Italian.
6 It was an incredible experience!
7 She lives in a really attractive area.
8 I'll phone for an ambulance immediately.

4 A ends in a consonant sound.
B begins with a vowel sound.

5 2 It was‿an‿easy exam.
3 The weather was‿absolutely awful!
4 He got‿into their‿office‿easily.
5 She speaks‿excellent‿English‿and‿Italian.
6 It was‿an‿incredible‿experience!
7 She lives‿in‿a really attractive‿area.
8 I'll phone for‿an‿ambulance immediately.

Unit 14

Problem consonants: /tʃ/, /dʒ/, and /j/

3 1 /tʃ/   5 /dʒ/   9 /dʒ/
2 /j/   6 /tʃ/   10 /dʒ/
3 /tʃ/   7 /j/
4 /j/   8 /dʒ/

4 1   /j/   yoga, yacht, yoghurt
2 a /dʒ/ jacket, jeans
2 b /dʒ/ gin, geography
3   /tʃ/ chocolate, chimpanzee, chess

Words with similar vowel sounds

2 1 leave   5 were   9 walk
2 where   6 want   10 live
3 this   7 hungry 11 angry
4 won't   8 work   12 these

▶ T14.4
A Right, so we've got twelve boxes …
B Yeah.
A … and twelve words.
B Right.
A … and I've got to put the right word in each box.
B That's it.
A Ok, so tell me, what's number one?
B Number one is … *leave* … that's right, *leave*.
A *Leave* is number one … OK, so where's *live*?
B That's … er … number ten.
A *Live* is number ten, OK. And *want* and *won't*, where are they?
B Well, *want* is number six …
A Number six *want*, yeah.
B … and *won't* is number four.
A OK … what else is there … ah yes, *this*, where's *this*?
B *This* is number three …
A Yeah.
B … and *these* is number twelve.
A *These* is number twelve. OK, so what's number two then?
B Number two is *where*.
A *Where* is number two … right, so what else …
B Well, number eight is *work*.
A *Work* is number eight, yeah?
B And number nine is *walk*.
A *Work* and *walk*, eight and nine. OK, which leaves … ah yes, *hungry* and *angry* …
B Oh right, yes, so … *hungry* is number seven …
A Number seven *hungry*, right …
B … and *angry* is number eleven, at the bottom.
A And that's it …
B No, no … one more … *were*.
A Ah yes, *were* … so that must be number five, yes?
B That's it … *were* is number five. Yes.
A And that's it!

Contractions and weak forms in the Present Perfect

1 The correct sentences are:
1 a 2 b 3 b 4 a 5 a 6 a 7 b 8 b

3 the Colosseum, gondolas, the Leaning Tower of Pisa, the Pope

4 *have* or *has*   ✓✓✓✓
  've or *'s*   ✓✓✓✓✓
  haven't or *hasn't*   ✓✓

▶ T14.7
G Hello, Henry!
H George! How are you?
G Fine! We've just come back from our holiday!
H Yes?
G Yes! We've been to Italy! Have you been there?
H Oh, yes, I have. I've been to Italy many, many times.
G Oh.
H I've seen the Colosseum.
G Oh.
H I've been in a gondola.
G Oh.
H And I've climbed the Tower of Pisa.
G Oh.
H Twice.
G Oh, no, we haven't done any of those things.
H No?
G But we have seen the Pope! Have you seen him?
H Er, no, I haven't.
G Ah!
H But my wife has.

6 This is a secret message. If you know all the phonemic symbols you don't need to study page fifty-seven again.

Key 63

Phonemic symbols

The correct words from the box for the symbols on page 57 are as follows:

1	pencil	23	jeans
2	bags	24	sings
3	ticket	25	tea
4	door	26	is
5	key	27	bed
6	Greece	28	hand
7	five	29	start
8	vocabulary	30	not
9	sit	31	your
10	lives	32	good
11	like	33	do
12	man	34	love
13	no	35	girl
14	hot	36	sister
15	read	37	day
16	we	38	go
17	yellow	39	why
18	three	40	down
19	that	41	noise
20	shoe	42	beer
21	television	43	hair
22	choose	44	tour

OXFORD
UNIVERSITY PRESS

Great Clarendon Street, Oxford OX2 6DP

Oxford University Press is a department of the University of Oxford.
It furthers the University's objective of excellence in research, scholarship,
and education by publishing worldwide in

Oxford New York

Auckland Cape Town Dar es Salaam Hong Kong Karachi
Kuala Lumpur Madrid Melbourne Mexico City Nairobi
New Delhi Shanghai Taipei Toronto

With offices in

Argentina Austria Brazil Chile Czech Republic France Greece
Guatemala Hungary Italy Japan Poland Portugal Singapore
South Korea Switzerland Thailand Turkey Ukraine Vietnam

OXFORD and OXFORD ENGLISH are registered trade marks of
Oxford University Press in the UK and in certain other countries

© Oxford University Press 2002

The moral rights of the author have been asserted

Database right Oxford University Press (maker)

First published 2002

2012 2011 2010 2009 2008
10 9 8 7

No unauthorized photocopying

All rights reserved. No part of this publication may be reproduced, stored in a retrieval system, or transmitted, in any form or by any means, without the prior permission in writing of Oxford University Press, or as expressly permitted by law, or under terms agreed with the appropriate reprographics rights organization. Enquiries concerning reproduction outside the scope of the above should be sent to the ELT Rights Department, Oxford University Press, at the address above

You must not circulate this book in any other binding or cover and you must impose this same condition on any acquirer

Any websites referred to in this publication are in the public domain and their addresses are provided by Oxford University Press for information only. Oxford University Press disclaims any responsibility for the content

ISBN: 978 0 19 437621 1

Printed in China

ACKNOWLEDGEMENTS

The authors would like to acknowledge their debt to the writers of various standard pronunciation reference books, especially:
Ann Baker *Introducing English Pronunciation*
A.C. Gimson *A Practical Course of English Pronunciation*
Joanne Kenworthy *Teaching English Pronunciation*
Colin Mortimer *Elements of Pronunciation*
P. Roach *English Phonetics and Phonology*

In addition, we would like to extend our thanks to everyone at Oxford University Press and to John and Liz Soars for their continuing inspiration.

Illustrations by: Adrian Barclay pp7, 15, 22, 41, 46; Joanna Kerr pp12, 23, 37, 45; Nigel Paige pp9, 11, 13, 14, 16, 17, 18, 19, 20, 22, 23, 24, 25, 26, 28, 29, 31, 32, 33, 35, 36, 37, 38, 39, 40, 44, 45, 46, 47, 48, 49, 51, 54, 55, 56; Harry Venning pp6, 10, 11, 27, 30, 52, 53

The publisher would like to thank the following for their kind permission to reproduce photographs: Corbis UK Ltd pp27 (girl), 33 (Jacqueline Kennedy/Bettmann), 34 (smiling man), 42 (Hollywood); Photodisc pp27 (boy), 42 (The White House, Statue of Liberty); Popperfoto pp33 (Mick Jagger, George Clooney), 34 (police search/Russell Boyce/Reuters); Rex Features pp33 (George Michael/Sinead Lynch), 34 (strike/Peter Brooker); Science Photo Library p42 (Earth/Tom Van Sant/Geosphere Project, Santa Monica); Stone p34 (fire-fighters/Arnulf Husmo); Telegraph Colour Library p34 (bride and groom/Michael Goldman); Topham Picturepoint p33 (John Lennon/AG. Sperenza, Julia Roberts/Keystone/Homann)

Design by: Susan Clarke